10 Minute Guide to Lotus Notes® for Windows™

Kate Barnes

que

A Division of Macmillan Computer Publishing
201 W. 103rd Street, Indianapolis, Indiana 46290 USA

1995 by Que Books

International Standard Book Number: 1-56761-176-1
Library of Congress Catalog Card Number: 93-70250

97   96   10   9

Interpretation of the printing code: the rightmost double-digit number is the year of the book's printing; the rightmost single-digit number is the number of the book's printing. For example, a printing code of 93-1 shows that the first printing of the book occurred in 1993.

Publisher: *Marie Butler-Knight*
Associate Publisher: *Lisa A. Bucki*
Managing Editor: *Elizabeth Keaffaber*
Development Editor: *Seta Frantz*
Manuscript Editor: *Audra Gable*
Interior Design: *Amy Peppler-Adams*
Cover Design: *Dan Armstrong*
Indexer: *Jeanne Clark*
Production Team: *Diana Bigham, Scott Cook, Tim Cox, Mark Enochs, Tom Loveman, Carrie Roth, Barbara Webster*

Special thanks to Stephen Londergan for ensuring the technical accuracy of this book.

Screen reproductions in this book were created by means of the program Collage Plus from Inner Media, Inc., Hollis, NH.

Printed in the United States of America

Contents

Introduction

Do the following symptoms seem familiar?

- Pain as you sit through inefficient status meetings.

- Anguish at knowing that data exists but you can't get at it.

- Distress from having needed information but no means to share the information.

- Strain of both a personal and environmental nature as you pass paper within and between organizations.

If you are a sufferer of any of these symptoms of cumbersome information management, Notes is here to soothe and relieve. With Lotus Notes, working in a group is streamlined and improved. Notes is a remedy for meetings that waste time, processes that are paper intensive, communication breaks, and a host of other ailments common in most organizations.

Just What Is Lotus Notes?

Notes has been called "workgroup software" as well as an "information manager for groups." It was designed to aid work done by groups. With it, you and members of your group can develop documents and collect information from a variety of sources. Common formats that facilitate sharing and information retrieval are designed specifically for your group.

Common applications of Notes include:

- Development, approval, and management of administrative functions (such as travel authorizations and time reporting).

- Organization of product information.

- Customer support.

- Project tracking.

- Access and broadcast of information from outside databases.

These are just some of the possibilities. The Notes applications for *your* work group will be specific to the organization and communication needs of the group.

Why the 10 Minute Guide to Lotus Notes?

The *10 Minute Guide to Lotus Notes* was developed for you, the person who uses Notes applications. Although the book touches on application development from the end-user view, the book is not meant for application developers.

Each lesson is designed to be completed in 10 minutes or less. Using this book, you can have Notes up and running in about four hours.

If you are just getting started, begin at the beginning of the book so you don't miss a thing. Once you have become familiar with Notes, keep the *10 Minute Guide to Lotus Notes* handy to use as a quick refresher. Because the *10 Minute Guide to Lotus Notes* is efficient, we've used the front and back covers for important information. Don't miss them.

Conventions Used in this Book

This book assumes that you are using either Microsoft Windows or OS/2's Presentation Manager. Appendix A of this book lists some Windows basics for the beginner. This book also assumes that you are using a mouse with your system, although keyboard steps are given wherever they might be more convenient.

To help you move through the lessons easily, these conventions are used:

On-screen text	On-screen text will appear in a special computer font.
What you type	Information you type will appear in bold, color, computer font.
Items you select	Commands, options, and icons you select or keys you press will appear in color.
Selection keys	Boldface letters within a menu title, menu option, or dialog option indicate selection keys for keyboard shortcuts. These correspond to the underlined letters on-screen.

In addition to these conventions, the *10 Minute Guide to Lotus Notes* uses the following icons to identify helpful information:

Plain English   New or unfamiliar terms are defined in (you got it) "plain English."

Timesaver Tips   Look here for ideas that cut corners and confusion.

Panic Button   This icon identifies areas where new users often run into trouble and offers practical solutions.

For More Information . . .

Notes will work with either Microsoft Windows or OS/2 Presentation Manager. It is assumed that you have a basic knowledge of how to navigate through the system that is used by your work group. If not, you may want to learn some basics before proceeding with Notes. The following books may be of help:

10 Minute Guide to Windows 3.1, by Kate Barnes, published by Que Books.

10 Minute Guide to OS/2 2.1, by Herb Tyson and Revised by Kelly Oliver, published by Que Books.

Trademarks

All terms mentioned in this book that are known to be trademarks or service marks are listed below. In addition, terms suspected of being trademarks or service marks have been appropriately capitalized. Que cannot attest to the accuracy of this information. Use of a term in this book should not be regarded as affecting the validity of any trademark or service mark.

Lotus, 1-2-3, Freelance Plus, and Lotus Notes are trademarks of Lotus Development Corporation.

Microsoft Windows and Microsoft Word are trademarks of Microsoft Corporation.

Lesson 1

Welcome to Notes

In this lesson, you will learn what you can do with Lotus Notes, and how to start up Notes, change your password, and make a quick exit.

What Notes Can Do for You!

Notes is a powerful communication and organization tool. It complements the software you are already using, while providing functions not available through project managers, databases, word processors, or spreadsheets.

With Notes, you can create, organize, and share data among several computers on a network. It has some of the same features as products you may already be familiar with, like a word processor, but its main strengths are its information sharing capabilities and its capability to manipulate data.

Imagine you've completed a simple travel report. Instead of filling out a paper form, you can complete the travel report on-line and electronically "mail" it to your manager. Your manager can approve the report electronically and send it on to the accounting department for speedy reimbursement. She can even view a report of all employee travel reports to help her budget for next year's travel.

1

Lotus Notes Limitations

Don't throw away the software you are using now for your daily reports and charts, because Lotus Notes does have some limitations. Let's get the bad news out of the way:

• Although Notes can be effectively used for managing project tasks, it does not produce Pert or Gantt charts.

• Notes allows you to look at the contents of stored information in customized screen displays. However, as a user, you do not have the ability to produce your own reports in the conventional sense.

• Though Notes has database-like features, it wasn't designed to maintain up-to-the-moment databases across long distances. A master database can be updated several times a day, but users at remote locations will not have up-to-the-moment accurate data.

• While Notes lets you update and attach responses to documents, it doesn't track the content of changes to documents. When a document is edited, the old document is simply replaced by the new. So don't toss your word processor if you need redline and strikeout to compare edited versions of a single document.

• Notes allows for simple calculations. But for complex calculations, hang on to your spreadsheet software. Then exchange data to and from Notes for use by your workgroup.

New to Networks?

When you first start using a network, all the new terms you hear may seem intimidating. Here's a brief rundown of the players. Notes is used where multiple computers are tied together to share information. Linked computers make up a *local area network (LAN)*. One or more computers in the LAN are called *servers*. They contain the main Notes program files and the data created through applications. Computers which link to a server to share files and data are called *workstations. LAN workstations* are linked by cables. *Dial-up (laptop) workstations* connect to a server via telephone lines. The *Administrator* is assigned the responsibility to make sure all the people, hardware, and software connect.

Your First Time with Notes

Before you start, Notes must be installed on your computer. The Notes Administrator may have already installed it. If not, see the inside front cover for the steps.

Once Notes is installed, gather the following information:

- Whether your computer is a local area network (LAN) workstation, or a dial-up (remote) workstation that connects via a modem over a phone line to a server.

- If you are a dial-up laptop user, the names of your mail server, mail file, and mail server phone number.

- Your User ID and password and whether it is on a diskette, file or on the server. The Notes Administrator may have assigned a temporary password which you'll need.

Don't Know? If you don't know this information, contact your Notes Administrator.

When you have the answers to those questions, follow these steps to start Notes:

1. Locate the Notes icon shown in Figure 1.1. (You may have to open a program group to find it.)

2. Double-click on the icon with the mouse to select it.

Double-Click? Program Group? If you're not familiar with these terms, you might want to learn a little more about the Windows or Presentation Manager environment before you try to use Notes. Appendix A provides a basic Windows education; if you're a Presentation Manager user, look to your documentation.

3. If the Notes Workstation Setup dialog box shown in Figure 1.2 appears, it begins answering the series of setup questions. You'll identify your workstation connection, specify your User ID and password location, and, if you have a remote workstation, provide information about your mail.

Lotus Notes

Figure 1.1 The Notes icon.

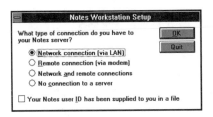

Figure 1.2   The Notes Setup dialog box.

When Notes starts, a screen similar to that shown in Figure 1.3 appears. You'll learn how to navigate this screen in the next lesson.

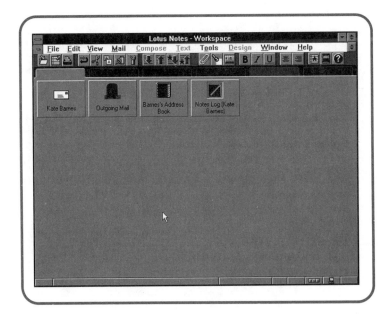

Figure 1.3   The Notes screen.

Changing Your Password

When you first start Notes, you use the temporary password that your Notes administrator assigned to you. You should change this temporary password to something that no one can guess. The following steps show you how to change your password.

Confused? These steps assume that you know how to use a pull-down menu system, which both Windows and Presentation Manager employ. If you're lost, review the Windows Primer in Appendix A.

1. Open the Tools menu by clicking on it or pressing Alt+O.

2. Click on User ID, Password, and then Set.

3. The Enter Password dialog box appears. Enter your current password and select OK.

4. In the Set Password dialog box, type a new password (31 characters or less in length). Pay attention to your use of uppercase and lowercase letters.

5. Select OK.

6. Enter the password a second time and select OK.

Leaving So Soon?

There is more than one way to exit Notes. Two simple ways are:

* Double-click on the Control Menu box

* Press Alt+F4

Another way is to leave Notes with the **File** menu. Follow these steps:

1. Open the **File** menu (click on it or press Alt+F).

2. Press X or click on Exit.

Haven't Saved Your Work? If you forget to save new or edited documents before exiting, Notes is watching out for you. A dialog box appears, asking whether you want to save each document. Respond Yes to save the work, No to lose the new work, or Cancel to cancel the Exit operation.

In this lesson, you learned what Notes can and can't do for you, as well as how to start and leave Notes. In the next lesson, you'll learn how to use what you see on-screen once Notes is started.

Lesson 2

Exploring Notes

In this lesson, you will explore the Notes screen and learn to access Help.

Once Notes has been successfully started, the workspace shown in Figure 2.1 appears. Let's take a few minutes to learn about the parts of the screen you see.

Looks Familiar?   Since Notes is designed to run in the Windows or Presentation Manager environment, many of its screen elements match those programs. Turn to Appendix A to learn about some of these common elements, such as scroll bars, Control Menu boxes, and pull-down menus.

Some Standard Sights You'll See

Figure 2.1 shows Notes running in a Windows environment. Some of the standard Windows features you see include:

Control Menu box   Click on this box to open the Control menu, from which you can size and reposition the window. Double-click on this box to exit Notes.

Control Menu box   Title bar   Minimize button

       Menu bar   SmartIcons   Maximize button

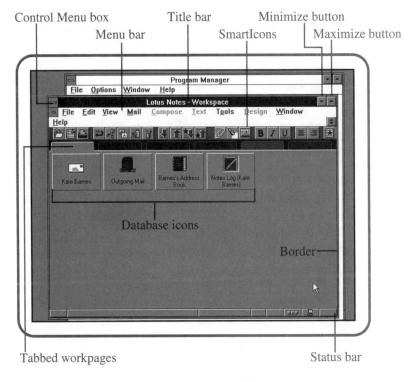

Tabbed workpages   Status bar

Figure 2.1   The Notes workspace.

Minimize and Maximize buttons   These arrows determine whether the window is maximized (full-screen size), minimized (reduced to an icon), or restored (open but less than full-screen size). To select any of these buttons, double-click on the button.

Border   The border defines the edge of the window. You can change the size of the window by dragging a border in any direction with the mouse.

Dragging with the Mouse To drag something with the mouse, place the mouse pointer on the item to drag. Press and hold the mouse button, and move the mouse to the new location. Then release the mouse button.

Scroll box, Scroll bar, Scroll button Sometimes the full contents of a window is not visible all at once, especially if the window is not maximized. The scroll box can be dragged with the mouse across the scroll bar to move through the contents of a window. You can scroll a small amount at a time by clicking with the mouse on a scroll button. The contents of the screen moves in the direction shown on the scroll button.

Menu bar and menus The menu bar displays the menu names you can select to access the commands contained in the menu. To select a menu command with the mouse, click on the menu name. The menu opens to display the available commands. To choose a command, click on the command.

Keyboard User? To use menus with the keyboard, press Alt to activate the menu bar. Then either use the arrow keys to move to the menu name you want and press Enter, or type the underlined letter in the menu name. Once the menu is open, use the arrow keys again to highlight the name of the command, or type the underlined letter in the command name.

Status bar   When you run Notes under Windows, the Status bar appears. It will inform you of fonts and text sizes, mail, and other conditions.

Special Notes Screen Features

In addition to the standard Windows or Presentation Manager interface, the Notes program offers some special on-screen features you need to know about.

Title Bar

If you use other Windows programs, the screen elements described so far probably seem familiar. With the title bar, Notes starts some new twists. When Notes is initially started, `Lotus Notes` appears in the title bar (see Figure 2.1). When a menu item is selected from the menu bar, a short description of the selection appears in the title bar. For example, in Figure 2.2, the menu item New Database is selected, and the description: `Create a new database and add it to your workspace` appears.

More Title Bar Uses   On dial-up workstations, the title bar is used to identify when communication is connected or disconnected. Also, the title bar can be used by the Notes Administrator to broadcast messages.

Description in Menu bar

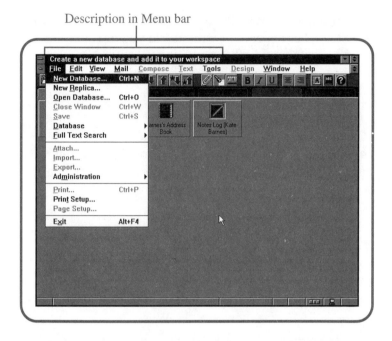

Figure 2.2 The title bar gives information about the highlighted command.

SmartIcons

SmartIcons are buttons you can customize to execute activities in Notes. Notes comes with several SmartIcons set up for you. To find out what each one does, point at it and hold down the right mouse button. Its function appears in the title bar. For example, the first SmartIcon shown in Figure 2.3 can be used to save a file.

In Lesson 15, you will learn how to select from over 100 SmartIcons supplied with Notes and how to create your own SmartIcons.

The File Save SmartIcon

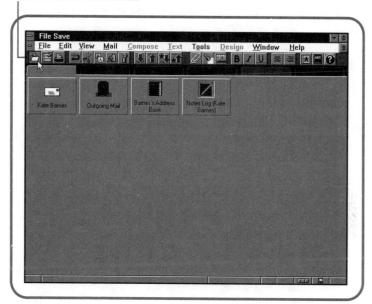

Figure 2.3 The File Save SmartIcon.

Database Icons

The database icons on the Notes workspace show each database's title and an identifying graphic. In the next lesson, you'll learn more about databases and how to use the database icons.

The Workspace and Tabbed Workpages

The workspace contains six tabbed workpages. You can assign colors and titles to the tabs and arrange related Notes database icons on a workpage.

For example, you may have three database icons for administrative functions, named Travel Report, Timesheet, and Leave Request. You could title one workpage "Adm" and place a database icon for each database on it. On a workpage you named "Clients," you could place databases called Client Tracking and Product Information.

To select a workpage, click on the tab with the mouse. The workpage selected comes to the front. Or press the up arrow key to highlight a workpage (see Figure 2.4), then use the left and right arrow keys to move from workpage to workpage.

To name and control the color of a workpage:

1. Double-click on the tab for the workpage or highlight the workpage and press Enter. The Workspace Page Name dialog box appears (see Figure 2.4).

2. Enter the Name for the workpage tab and/or select a Color.

3. Choose OK.

To move a database icon to a new workpage with the mouse, drag the database icon to the tab of the workpage. If you are using the keyboard, select the database icon with the arrow keys, then press Shift+Ctrl+arrow key until the destination workpage is highlighted. Release the keys and press Enter.

No Room in the Workpage? If the workpage appears full, don't worry. When it "fills up" on your screen, the workpage "expands" to accommodate new database icons. A scroll bar appears to allow you to view all the database icons on the workpage.

Workpage highlight

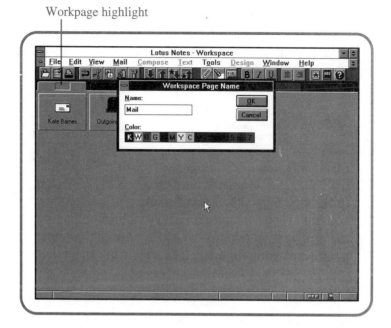

Figure 2.4   The Workspace Page Name dialog box.

Using Help

Although this book covers the basics, you can also turn to Notes for help. You can press F1 at any time to get help regarding your current activity. Figure 2.5 shows help on the Notes Workspace. Or, select **H**elp in the Menu Bar.

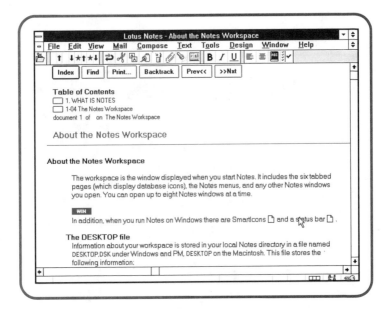

Figure 2.5 Help on the Notes Workspace.

The Help options follow:

Current Task	To get help on the current operation.
Table of Contents	To see and select from the Help Table of Contents.
Keyboard	To learn what keys to use for common tasks.
Messages	To gain information about Notes messages.
@Functions	To learn more about Notes predefined @ functions (which are used in macros).

16

Index
To see and select from the Help Index.

Using...
To look at a description of the selected database.

About...
To check out the purpose or policy of the selected database.

Release Notes
To examine information about the release of Notes you're using.

About Notes
To see the detail on the version of Notes you're using.

Help is actually a database in itself, like the other databases you work with in Lotus Notes. Although database activities are covered in greater depth in future chapters, here are some hints to familiarize you with Help.

When a Help command displays a list of topics, double-click on your selection, or highlight it and press Enter. Help text will appear for the topic you selected, and you'll see these buttons:

Index
Shows an index of the document if available.

Find
Allows you to enter text to find in the document.

Print
Allows you to print the document.

Backtrack   Returns you to the previous
                          window display.

Prev<<   Goes to the previous docu-
                          ment in the list.

>>Next   Goes to the next document
                          in the list.

When you want to leave Help, just close each window you've opened by pressing Ctrl+F4 or double-clicking on the Control Menu box.

In this lesson, you learned how to get around the Notes screen and get help. In the next lesson, you'll begin learning all about using databases and learn more about the concepts we've touched on as you learned how to use the Help database.

Lesson 3

Using a Database

In this lesson, you will learn about handling database icons, as well as opening, copying, and closing a database and stopping an operation in progress.

Databases and Their Contents

Before we get too far into Notes, it's important that you know about Notes databases, documents, forms, and views.

A *database* groups related information. It contains *documents*, *forms*, and *views*. A document is a single entry in a database. A document may be lengthy (such as a complex report including graphics) or short (like a quick reply to an inquiry). You'll use forms to enter information into documents as well as to display and print the information. You'll use views to find documents. Views let you list available documents in a variety of ways.

A *database icon* is a symbol that represents a particular database. The database itself resides on the server, but the icon appears on your own workpage, providing you with an easy way to access the database's contents.

Adding a Database Icon to Your Workspace

Although your server may hold many databases, only the ones you pick will appear as icons in your workspace. That way, your workspace does not become cluttered with icons for databases that you seldom use.

No Access? Databases stored on your or anyone else's hard disk cannot be accessed by others. You may access databases on the server or on your local hard disk

The following steps add a database icon for an existing database to the active (top) workpage. Make sure you activate the desired workpage (see Lesson 2) before you start these steps.

Let's Talk Simple! From now on in this book, I'll assume that you know how to use Notes' menus. For example, in step 1 below, "Select File Open Database" means to open the File menu and then select the Open Database command. For more information on menus, see Appendix A.

1. Select File Open Database (or press Ctrl+O). The Open Database dialog box appears as in Figure 3.1. Notice that available Server(s) appear. (*Local* is the term used for your hard disk.)

2. To see the databases available on a server, double-click on the server name (or highlight it and select Open). The descriptive titles of the database on the server appear, as does the Filename of the selected database.

3. Highlight the name of the database to add to your workpage. (If your computer is set up to use a modem to call the selected server, you must select Call.)

4. Select Add Icon to add the database icon and return to the workpage. To add the database icon and open the database, double-click on the name or highlight it and select Open.

5. When you have added all the database icons you need, select Done.

Figure 3.1   The Open Database dialog box.

Look Before You Leap   To make sure you are adding the *correct* database icon, you can select About from the Open Database dialog box to see a description of the database.

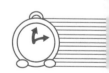

Adding More Than One?   If you want to add database icons to several workpages, it may be most efficient to add all the database icons to a single workpage from the Open Database dialog box. Then move icons individually to the their proper workpages.

21

Not all servers and databases are available to all users. If you cannot find a database, contact the Lotus Notes Administrator and see whether you are set up to access that database. Further, although the database may appear in the Open Database dialog box, your access may be limited. Your Lotus Notes Administrator can advise you on changing access capabilities.

Opening a Database in the Workspace

Once you've added a database icon to your workspace, all you have to do is double-click on the database icon to open the database. Or you can type the first letter of the database name as needed to highlight the database icon, and press Enter.

When you open a database, the workspace typically displays the database's policy document (Figure 3.2), a Help screen that tells you how to use the database you've opened.

 **What Was That Again?** If you want to view the policy document again later, select Help Using. You can select Help About to see the description of the database.

Close the Help screen by double-clicking on the Control Menu box, and the database itself will appear. Figure 3.3 shows a view of a database called Contract Library. In this view, a resignation letter document is highlighted.

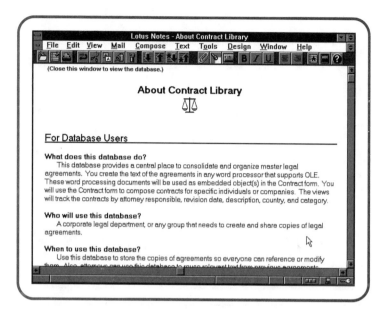

Figure 3.2 Database policy document.

Database Information

From time to time, you may need some basic information about a database, such as the creation date, last modification date, size, number of documents, and title. For example, you might need to know the size of a database before copying it to a floppy disk. To show this database information, follow these steps:

1. Select the database icon.

2. Select File Database Information.

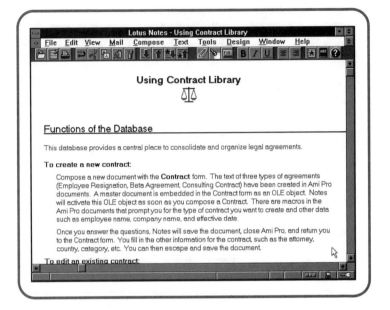

Figure 3.3 Database view with resignation document highlighted.

Closing a Database

To close a database, press Esc or Ctrl+W. Or select File Close Window or double-click the right mouse button. Each time you do this, one database window is closed. Continue until all windows are closed, and you are returned to the workpage.

Copying a Database

With appropriate access you may be able to copy an entire database (including forms, views, and documents) to make a backup copy of it on another disk. Or you may want to copy just the forms and views to use as a basis for a new database. To copy a database:

1. Highlight the desired database's icon.

2. Select File Database Copy. The Database Copy dialog box appears (see Figure 3.4).

3. Choose the Server where the database should be stored, enter the Filename (up to 8 characters), and enter a Title for the database.

4. Choose the appropriate radio button for what you want to copy: Forms, Views, and Documents, or Forms and Views Only.

5. Select New Copy.

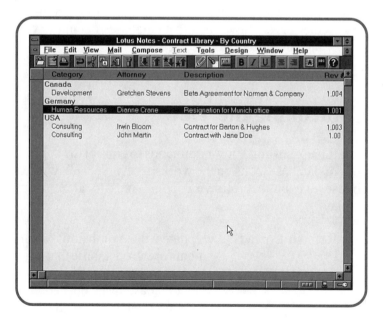

Figure 3.4   The Database Copy dialog box.

Removing a Database Icon

If you no longer want a database icon to appear on your workpage, you can remove it with these steps:

1. Select the icon you want to remove.

2. Press Delete.

3. A dialog box with the message Remove selected icon(s) from your workspace? appears.

4. Select Yes to remove the icon or No if you've changed your mind.

Don't Mess with Database Files Deleting a database icon from your workpage does not remove the database itself. The database remains on the server. Never delete a database file unless you are sure it will not be needed.

Controlling the View

You can use several View commands to control the appearance of database icons on the workspace. Select View, then choose one of the following commands to affect your display.

Refresh Unread   Updates the number of documents in each database that have gone unread since the last time the database was opened and displays the number in the database icon.

Arrange Icons	Arranges database icons in rows.
Show Unread	Displays in each database's icon the number of unread documents in that database.
Show Server Names	Displays the server name in the database's icon.

In this lesson, you learned how to control database icons, how to open, copy, and close a database, and how to stop an operation in progress. In the next lesson, you'll learn more about Notes views.

Viewing and Selecting

In this lesson, you will learn how to use Notes' viewing options and how to select documents from a database.

Database Views

As you may remember from Lesson 3, a database can contain multiple views. A view determines how the documents are displayed. Views can display all documents or only selected documents in the database, and can sort the document listing by a variety of criteria. Views differ from database to database. Figure 4.1 shows one view of a database. Here, documents are displayed by country.

Changing a View

The view that appears is the last view that was used. You will want to change views to sort information in a different order or to see different information about the documents in the database. To change the view, follow these steps:

1. From an open database, select View. The View menu shown in Figure 4.2 appears. The available views appear at the bottom of the menu. Here the By Country view has been selected and is the current view.

2. Select a new view. The menu closes and the new view appears.

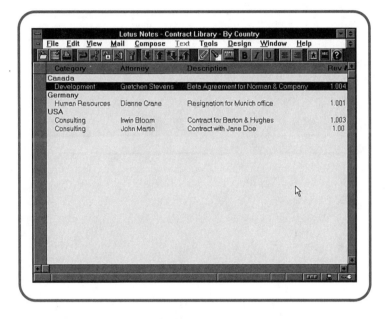

Figure 4.1 A database view where the documents are displayed by country.

Keep the Document To track a document from one view to the next, highlight the document and hold down Ctrl when you switch to the next view. The document remains highlighted in the new view.

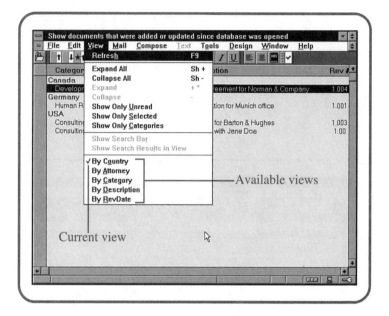

Figure 4.2 The View menu with By Country selected.

Refreshing Your View

When you or other users add or delete documents from a database, the view is not automatically updated to reflect the change. Choose View Refresh (or press F9) to refresh the view. (Closing and reopening the database also refreshes the view, but is more time consuming.)

Expanding and Collapsing Views

The level of detail shown in a view can be expanded or collapsed. In a collapsed view, you see the various categories of documents in the database; in an expanded view, you can see and select from the actual documents.

Categories? A category is a name used to group related documents in a view. Categories and subcategories are referred to as having levels which reflect the amount of detail displayed.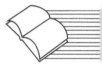

For example, Figure 4.3 shows an expanded view of the Help database Table of Contents view. It includes documents and subcategories. Figure 4.4 shows a collapsed view. Notice that documents and subcategories are hidden.

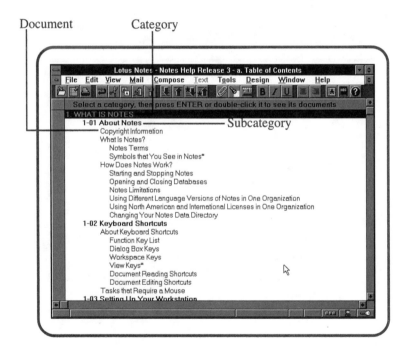

Figure 4.3 The Help database Table of Contents view expanded.

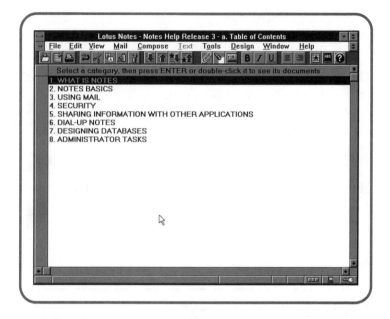

Figure 4.4 Help database Table of Contents view collapsed.

Use the actions in Table 4.1 to expand or collapse views. You can perform most of the actions by either selecting from a menu or pressing a key combination.

Gray Keys Are Special Do not confuse the gray Plus and Minus keys on the right end of the keyboard with the regular Plus and Minus keys above the letter P. Use the gray keys for expanding and collapsing.

Table 4.1 Expanding and collapsing a view.

Expand Action	Menu Selection	Keys
A level in category	-	Gray Plus
All levels in category	-	Gray *
All levels/all categories	View, Expand All	Shift+Plus
Collapse Action	Menu Selection	Keys
All levels in category	-	Shift+Gray Minus
All levels/all categories	View, Collapse All	Shift+Minus

Highlight First   When expanding or collapsing for a single category, make sure the highlight is within the category.

Selecting Documents

You can manually or automatically select documents and categories in a view. Once documents and categories are selected, you can act upon them: you can compose a response, print, forward through the mail, delete, and so on.

Manual Selection

To manually select a single document, do one of the following:

- Highlight the document and press Spacebar.

- Or use the mouse to click in the left margin next to the document.

To manually select a consecutive group of documents:

- Hold down Shift+Spacebar and use the arrow keys to highlight the group.

- Or drag the mouse in the left margin. When a document or category is selected, a check mark appears to its left.

To deselect a document, perform the same actions you did to select it. The check mark will disappear.

Use a combination of single document selection and consecutive group selection to choose a group of documents that are not contiguous.

Automatically Select All

If you want to select many categories and documents, it might be faster to select all of them, and then deselect the few that you don't want. From the view, choose Edit Select All (or press Ctrl+A).

Whenever at least one category or document is selected, you can choose to deselect everything. Choose Edit Deselect All.

Automatic Selection by Date

Sometimes you might want to select documents that have a certain date or range of dates. To do so, follow these steps:

1. Deselect all documents (using Edit Deselect All).

2. Choose Edit Select by Date.

3. In the Select by Date dialog box, enter the From (beginning date) and the To (ending date). Also indicate whether you want Notes to look at the dates when the document was Created or last Modified.

4. Select OK when you are done. The number of documents selected appears on the status bar in the lower left corner of the window.

Dating   When you enter the date in Windows, use MM/DD/YY. If you are working under Presentation Manager, use MM-DD-YY. Using either, you can also enter times with Yesterday and Today such as "8:00 Yesterday."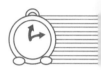

Automatic Selection with Find

One way to automatically select documents (not categories) is to find and mark documents in the current view which contain given text. The following steps show you how.

1. Select Edit Find or press Ctrl+F. The Options Find dialog box appears.

2. Enter the text to locate in the Find text box.

3. Complete the dialog box by marking any check boxes desired and selecting the appropriate radio button.

4. Choose the Find All button and the selections are marked. (If no occurrence of the text was found, a dialog box appears to let you know.)

That's Not What I Saw If you used the Edit Find command and saw the Query Builder dialog box instead of the Options Find dialog box, your database is set up for searching full text. You'll learn about this in the next lesson; be patient until then.

Limiting the View

Once documents and/or categories are selected, you can limit the view to your selections. You can further limit the view by showing only unread documents or only certain categories.

To Read or Not To Read A *read* document is one that you have opened. *Unread* documents can be denoted differently in different databases. For example, an unread document might have a star icon to the left of the document in the view, or the document might appear in another color. How unread documents appear in the view is determined by the designer of the database.

Follow these steps to limit the view:

1. Select View. The Show Only options appear. When an option is selected, it appears with a check mark in front of it.

2. Select one of the following options, and the specified documents are immediately displayed:

   Show Only Unread displays only the documents not read.

Show Only Selected displays documents that were selected.

Show Only Categories hides all documents and displays only the categories.

In this lesson, you learned how to change the view of a database by selecting a new view or changing the appearance of a view already selected. You also learned how to refresh views and select documents and categories. In the next lesson, you'll learn how to use Notes' search feature to perform searches with sophisticated criteria you've set.

Lesson 5

Searching Documents from Views

In this lesson, you will learn how to search documents from views.

Searching Documents

In Lesson 4, you learned how to find consecutive text. You can also perform full text searches, which means that you can find documents containing words, parts of words, phrases, numbers, or dates which are not consecutive. You can also perform more complex queries such as searching out documents using operators such as AND, OR, and NOT. For example, you could find a document with the following types of combinations:

- "Patterson" AND "Dart" (Will find "Jay Patterson and Julie Dart." Both words must appear.)

- "Patterson" OR "Dart" (Will find "Jay Patterson and Julie Dart." Either word will appear.)

- "Patterson" NOT "Dart" (Will not find "Jay Patterson and Julie Dart." One word must appear, but the other must not.)

But I Can't To perform a full text search, the database must be set up with full text index (on the server or locally). If it is not, the menu options discussed in this section are grayed-out and can't be used. If you want a database set up with a full text index, contact your Notes Administrator for more information.

Once selected, the search bar appears below the menu bar. Figure 5.1 shows the search bar. To make selections from the search bar, click on it with the mouse and enter the text for which you want to search. Or use Shift+F6 to move between the search bar and the rest of the window. When in the search bar, use Tab to move between the options and press Enter to choose an option.

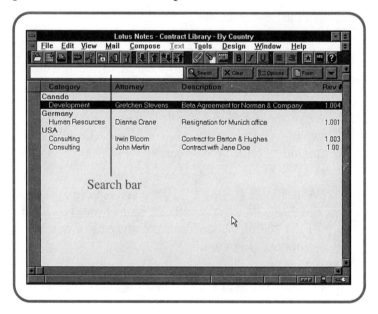

Figure 5.1 The search bar appears when you select View Show Search Bar.

Performing a Simple Search

When you enter words or phrases for which to search, there are a few rules to follow. You can use a question mark as a single unknown character or an asterisk to identify one or more unknown characters. For example, "d?t" will match "dot" but not "delight." The entry "d*t" will match both "dot" and "delight." Phrases with several words must be entered in quotation marks, as in "Brown and Black Company."

To perform a simple search, select the view showing the documents to search then follow these steps:

1. In the search bar text box, type the word or phrase.

2. Select the Search button.

3. The document(s) that contain the search text appear in the view with a gray bar to the left of the document name.

4. You can see the search result in the view by selecting View, Show Search Results in View. (Deselect this command to return to the earlier view.)

When Will It Stop? If you are searching a large database, the search will take some time. The length of the search depends on the amount of text to be searched. Be patient.

To clear the result of the search, select the Clear button.

Searching Several Databases You may want to search for a word or phrase in several databases. You could search each one individually. However, it is faster to select each database from the workspace, then choose Edit Find. Select each database to display all views. Then perform the search using the search bar.

Setting Search Options

Before performing a search, you can set search options to define the search more precisely. From the search bar, select the Options button. The Search Options dialog box, shown in Figure 5.2, appears.

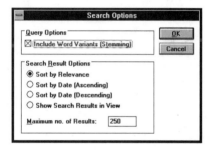

Figure 5.2   The Search Options dialog box.

Check Include Word Variants (Stemming) under Query Options if you want to search out words where your entry may be the stem.

The Stem   The *stem* of a word refers to only a portion of the word. For example, you may want to enter "contract" as a stem and have the search yield words like "contracts" and "contracting."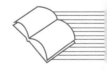

Next select one of the Search **R**esult Options described here:

Sort by Relevance   Documents are sorted by the directness of their relationship to the query.

Sort by Date (Ascending)   Documents are sorted by date of last modification with the oldest document first.

Sort by Date (Descending)   Documents are sorted by date of last modification with the newest document first.

Show Search Results in View   Documents are shown in the current view with a check mark by those selected in the search.

Finally, you can indicate the **M**aximum Number of Results you want to find. This is important if you are searching a common occurrence through many documents but only want a sampling. Select OK to close the dialog box, then perform the search. In the search bar text box, type the word or phrase and select the Search button.

Performing a Query

To use the advanced full text query features, select Edit Find. If the full text index is enabled for the database (see your Notes Administrator), the Query Builder dialog box shown in Figure 5.3 appears. (If not, the simpler version covered in Lesson 4 appears.)

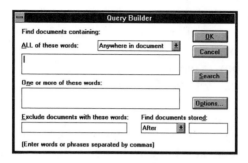

Figure 5.3   The Query Builder dialog box.

There are three text boxes where you can enter words or phrases. When you enter words or phrases, separate each by a comma. You can query for:

ALL of these words   This is the AND function. The search will only find documents containing every word or phrase listed here.

One or more of these words   This is the OR function. The search will find documents with any combination of these words or phrases.

Exclude documents with these words   This is the NOT function. The search will not select documents which contain one or more of these words.

There are two drop-down list boxes on the Query Builder dialog box. In the first, you can specify that the words or phrases can be found Anywhere in document. The alternative (Near each other) limits the search to finding words and phrases that Notes determines are near each other.

In the other drop-down list box, you can indicate that you want to Find documents store**d** After or Before the date you enter in the text box that follows this drop-down list box. You do not have to enter a date if you don't want the search to be date-sensitive.

If you want to set search options, select the Options button. The same Search Options dialog box described earlier appears. Otherwise, select Search to begin the search. When the search is complete, Notes displays the documents which contain the specified text. The selection criteria also appears in the Search bar text box.

In this lesson, you learned how to perform simple searches and more complex queries. In the next lesson, you'll learn about other activities that can be handled from a view.

Lesson 6

Manipulating Documents from a View

In this lesson, you will learn how to work with documents from the view. You'll learn to copy, delete, and categorize documents within the view, as well as to print the view.

Copy Documents

At any given time, you might need to create another version of a document or create a new document that is substantially like an existing one. To do this, you can copy documents to the Clipboard and then paste the documents in the same view.

The Clipboard The *Clipboard* is a temporary storage area. When you copy material to the Clipboard, that material replaces any material which was currently in the Clipboard. The Clipboard is cleared when you exit Windows or Presentation Manager.

45

Copying a document places a duplicate of it in the Clipboard, leaving the original in place. To copy one or more documents, follow these steps:

1. Select the document(s) to copy, as you learned in Lesson 4.

2. Choose Edit Copy (or press Ctrl+C). The document(s) are placed in the Clipboard.

3. Select Edit Paste (or press Ctrl+V). The documents in the Clipboard appear in the view.

Notes automatically places the documents in the appropriate categories. The documents you copied were categorized in the view before the copy operation; therefore, they continue to appear in the view after the copy.

Printing a View

In this lesson, we're working with views rather than individual documents, but the procedures for printing a view and for printing a document are nearly the same.

You'll learn more about printing documents later in the book, but for now, let's print a copy of the view.

1. If desired, select the categories and documents to print.

2. Select File Print (or press Ctrl+P).

3. In the File Print dialog box (shown in Figure 6.1), enter the number of Copies, the Page Range, and whether you want to print in Draft Quality. Then select the radio button Print View.

4. Select OK. A message appears indicating that the output is being sent to the printer.

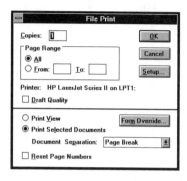

Figure 6.1 The File Print dialog box.

Printing Documents You may also print complete documents from the view by selecting the Print Selected Documents radio button. This option and other document print options are covered in greater detail in Lesson 8.

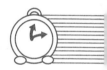

It Didn't Work If your printer did not produce the print, your printer may not be set up properly. Consult Lesson 8 for more information.

Deleting Documents

Within a view and the proper security, you can mark documents to be deleted. The documents are actually deleted when you leave the database.

To mark a document for deletion, first make sure that no documents are selected in the view. Then highlight the document and press Delete. A trash can icon appears next to the document. To undelete, highlight the document and press Delete again. The trash can disappears.

You can also mark multiple documents to be deleted. Follow these steps:

1. Select the documents. (You can collapse categories once the documents are selected in the category—the documents stay selected.)

2. Press Delete or select Edit Clear. The dialog box shown in Figure 6.2 appears.

3. The number of documents marked to clear is identified. To delete all documents, select All Checked. To delete only those checked documents you can see in the view, select Only Current. To stop the operation, select Cancel.

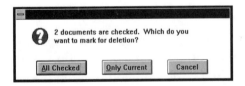

Figure 6.2   The dialog box to mark multiple documents for deletion.

Remember, documents are not deleted until you close the database. To remove the trash can symbols from multiple files:

1. Select the documents to undelete. (The document will now have both a trash can and a check mark to the left.)

2. Select Edit Undo Delete (or press Ctrl+Z). The dialog box appears.

3. To undelete all documents, select All Checked. To remove the trash cans for only those checked documents you can see in the view, select Only Current.

When you close the database, a message like the following appears:

```
Delete the 2 marked document(s) permanently
from the database Contract Library?
```

Respond Yes to delete the documents or No to keep the documents and remove the deletion marks.

Goodbye Category   If you delete all the documents from a category, the category itself is also deleted. Otherwise, categories are not affected by deletion activities.

Categorizing Documents in the View

To keep your documents organized, you can create categories and assign documents to them. To create a new category for documents, follow these steps:

1. Select the document(s) to categorize.

2. Choose Tools Categorize. The Categorize dialog box appears.

3. In New Categories, enter one or more new category name(s). If you enter multiple category names, separate them with a comma.

4. Select OK.

5. The view reappears with the documents in the category.

New Categories and Documents Unless you have a fairly high access level, you must have a document to assign to a new category before you can create that category.

Except When... The view must sort and categorize on a field called Categories. (This is a criteria set up during the design of the database. Not all views allow categorization. If your view doesn't allow it, Notes will let you know with a message, and you will not be able to categorize. To check out categorization, try your mail database.)

To assign documents to existing categories, follow these steps:

1. Select the document(s) to categorize.

2. Choose Tools Categorize. The Categorize dialog box appears.

3. In the Categorize dialog box, select one or more categories you want the documents to appear under.

4. Select OK.

5. The view reappears with the documents in the category.

Subcategory Please   Subcategories don't appear in the dialog box. To place the documents under a subcategory, type in the category, a backslash, then the subcategory in the New Categories text box (for example, RESOURCES\OFFICE SPACE).

In this lesson, you learned how to copy and delete documents in the view, how to print the view, and how to change categories. In the next lesson, you will learn about how to work with documents themselves.

Lesson 7

Using
Documents

In this lesson, you will learn how to create a document and how to work with and navigate existing documents.

Each Notes database is designed to hold certain types of information. When you create a document in Notes, you'll work in a database specifically designed for the required information, and you will use a form that helps you enter the information in the right format.

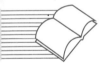

Forms of Forms Each database has one or more *forms* for creating new documents. Each form has a set layout including *fields* for entering information and, possibly, selections from which to choose.

The database designer and the clients (those who will be using the database) develop the forms for entering data, the views for document display, and the structure of the database itself. The information in a document may include numbers, words, graphics, portions of spreadsheets—virtually any computer-based information.

A Look at an Example Form

Figure 7.1 shows a sample form for entering contract information. The form contains several types of fields including *keyword fields*. Because the spelling and entry of keywords is controlled to provide structure to the database, keyword fields are usually presented as options from which to choose.

Why Keywords Are the Key *Keywords* are words or phrases identified by the database designer and client to define how data is related. For example, a keyword for a sales document might be Area, for which there are three values: North, South, and Central. No other value is allowed, because data could not be located later.

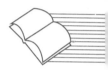

In Figure 7.1, the Attorney field appears as a series of radio buttons from which only one alternative may be selected. Another keyword field on this form is the Agreement Category. The possible Agreement Categories are preset to fit in the current categories for the view. When the user types in a first letter, like H for Human Resources, the category appears.

As you move from field to field, prompts appear at the bottom of the screen to identify what you should enter in each field. If you are trying to enter data where it cannot be entered, a message like the following will appear:

```
This is the protected area of the form.
```

If you try to enter data where a certain value must be entered, you may hear a beep until you enter a valid value.

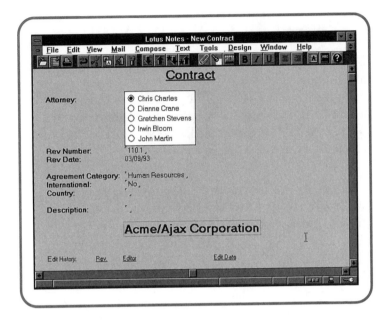

Figure 7.1 The Contract form.

Select a Document First Some forms are called *response forms* and must be linked to another document. When you use a response form, select the document to which you are responding, then choose Compose, Response.

Creating a New Document

To select and complete a form (thus creating a document), follow these steps:

1. Select the appropriate database. (Ask your Notes Administrator for assistance if you're not sure.)

2. Select Compose.

3. Choose the form you want to use. (Again, ask for help if you're not sure which form is the right one.) The form appears in a window, with its name at the top. Names of fields are followed by data that has been entered or by a bracketed area in which you enter information. (Refer again to Figure 7.1.)

4. Complete the fields (see the next section).

Entering Information Into Fields

To move from field to field, click on a field or use the Tab key. Use the arrow keys to move around in a field. To enter information, just type it. If text exists, the text you type is added at the insertion point. To type over existing information, select the text first, then type over it. (The next section describes how to select text.)

Deleting and Editing Information

There are several ways to delete. You can press the Delete key to delete the character to the right of the insertion point or the Backspace key to delete the character to the left. You can also select text (see the next section) and press Delete to delete more than one character at a time.

If you make a change that you want to discard, select Edit Undo, press Ctrl+Z, or click on the Edit Undo SmartIcon. Any of these actions restores the text to its previous form.

Opening an Existing Document

The available existing documents are listed on the view. To open one of them, follow these steps:

1. From the view, highlight the document title and press Enter or double-click on the document title.

2. If you want to edit the document, press Ctrl+E or select Edit, Edit Document.

3. Edit, save, and close the document using the approaches described in this lesson.

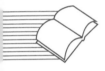 **Edit Mode and Read-Only Mode** When you enter an existing document, you are in *Read-Only mode*. This means that you may read the document, but you cannot make changes to the document. To edit the document you must invoke *Edit mode* by pressing Ctrl+E. You leave Edit mode by pressing Ctrl+E again.

Moving Within and Among Documents

You can use the scroll bars to move within the document to read or edit it. Or you can use the keyboard alternatives in Table 7.1 to move in a document.

Table 7.1 Moving within a document using the keyboard.

To move	Press
Page up or page down	PgUp or PgDn
Page right or page left	Home or End
Beginning of document	Ctrl+Home
End of document	Ctrl+End

Table 7.2 shows shortcuts for moving between documents from within a document.

Table 7.2 Moving between documents.

Key	SmartIcon	Action
Backspace	Navigate Prev	To go to the previous document in the view.
Enter	Navigate Next	To go to the next document in the view.
Shift+F4 or Shift+Tab	Navigate Prev Unread	To go to the previous unread document in the view.
F4 or Tab	Navigate Next Unread	To go to the next unread document in the view.
Shift+Enter		To display the first document in the next main topic.
Shift+ Backspace		To display the first document in the previous main topic.
F3		To display the next selected document.

Select Then Read   If you need to read several documents, here's a timesaver. Select each document to read from the view. Then open the first document, read it, and press F3 to continue to the next. Continue pressing F3 until all documents are read. This way, you don't have to return to the view between documents.

Selecting Text

When you want to perform the same action on many characters at once, it's efficient to select the whole block of text before you issue the command. For example, to delete a sentence, select the sentence, then press Delete.

To select text, click and drag the mouse or press and hold down Shift as you move with an arrow key. To deselect, click outside the field or use Shift+arrow key again. Table 7.3 shows ways to quickly select text.

Table 7.3   Selecting text.

Activity	Action
Select a word	Double-click on a word or press Ctrl+Shift+arrow key on a word.
Select to end of line	Press Shift+End.
Select to start of line	Press Shift+Home.
Select to end of field	Press Ctrl+Shift+End.
Select to start of field	Press Ctrl+Shift+Home.
Select a field	Press Ctrl+A or select **Edit Select All.**

Activity	Action
Deselect text	Choose **Edit Deselect All**.
Select entire document	Open document and immediately select **Edit Select All**.

Saving Your Work (Without Exiting Notes)

One way to save a document is to exit the Notes program (see Lesson 1). When you exit, Notes asks you if you want to save your work. But if you are not finished using Notes, you'll want to save *without* exiting. There are two ways of doing this:

- If you created a new document, select File Save (or press Ctrl+S or select the File Save SmartIcon).

- If you're editing a document, select Edit, Edit Document (or press Ctrl+E).

  If a message appears asking you to confirm the save, answer **Yes**.

Marking a Document for Deletion

In Lesson 6, you learned how to mark documents for deletion from the view. You can also mark a document for deletion from within the document itself. To do so, follow these steps:

1. Make sure you are not in Edit mode (select Ctrl+E to leave Edit mode, if necessary).

2. Press Delete or select the Edit Clear SmartIcon. A trash can is placed to the left of the document name in the view, and you are taken to the next document in the view.

   To undelete the document without going to the view:

1. Press Backspace. The document marked for deletion appears.

2. Press Delete again or select Edit Undo Delete (or press Ctrl+Z).

For more information about controlling documents marked for deletion from the view, see Lesson 6.

Closing a Document

After you save a document, it remains on-screen. To get a document out of your way when you're finished with it, you must close it. To close a document, follow these steps:

1. Choose File Close Window (or press Ctrl+W).

2. If information is required in the document before you save it, a message appears. Complete the information.

3. If changes were made in the document that were not saved, a message appears asking if you want to save changes. Respond Yes to save changes and exit the document. Respond No to leave the document without saving the changes. Choose Cancel to cancel the operation and remain in the document.

When you close a newly created document, its name is added to the view. When you close an existing document that was marked as unread, the unread marker disappears from the view for that document.

A Quick Out   A quick way to close a document is to press Esc or to double-click the right mouse button.

In this lesson, you learned how to create new documents, edit existing documents, and mark documents for deletion from within a document. In the next lesson, you will continue your work with documents by learning how to print a document.

Lesson 8
Printing

In this lesson, you will learn how to print and how to change settings which affect printing.

Printing a Document

Occasionally you will want to print documents in order to keep a paper record of them, to pass them on to someone who does not have access to Lotus Notes, or to take them with you when you work away from your terminal.

Are You Ready?   Before you print a document, make sure the printer is turned on and has plenty of paper available. If there is an "On-line" light on the printer, make sure it is lit. (Press the On-line button if the light is not lit.) In order to print, your workstation must be hooked up to a printer, and the appropriate printer driver must be installed through Windows or Presentation Manager. See "Choosing a Printer" later in this lesson if you run into problems getting the printed result you want.

You can print the current document (the document that's open), or you can select one or more documents from the view to print. You can even print the view itself, as described in Lesson 6.

To print the current document, follow these steps:

1. Select File Print or press Ctrl+P. The File Print dialog box shown in Figure 8.1 appears.

2. Enter the number of Copies. Enter whether you want to print All pages or a range From and To. Identify whether or not you want to print in Draft Quality. You can also select Setup to change printer settings. Setup options are covered later in this lesson.

3. Select OK when all settings have been chosen. A message appears indicating that the print is being sent to the printer. If you need to cancel the print job, select Cancel.

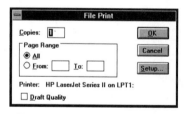

Figure 8.1   The File Print dialog box.

Choosing a Printer

If you have trouble printing, you may need to make sure the proper printer is selected. Or you may have more than one printer available for use and want to switch.

To choose a printer, select File Print Setup. On the Print Setup dialog box, select the printer to use and select OK. If the printer does not appear on the Print Setup dialog box or you want to change settings, select Setup. (The Setup options are described in the next section.)

Changing Printer Settings Through Setup

As we've seen, the Setup button is available from both the File Print dialog box and the Print Setup dialog box. When the button is chosen at either place, the dialog box shown in Figure 8.2 appears. The box you see may look a little different, depending on the type of printer you are using.

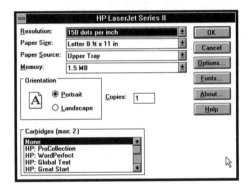

Figure 8.2 The setup dialog box for a LaserJet Series II printer. Yours will be different if you have a different printer.

There are a variety of options on the dialog box. Values were automatically entered by Notes for the printer. You can change settings that are different for your printer or your printing environment. Not all printers support all of the following options.

Resolution   Select the resolution for your printer. Typically, higher resolution means a higher quality print.

Paper Size   Select the size of paper you'll use.

Paper **S**ource   Identify where the paper will come from. For example, you can have an upper or lower tray on the printer or decide to manually feed the paper.

Memory   Identify the amount of memory in your printer.

Orientation   Select whether you want to print in **P**ortrait orientation (taller than wide) or **L**andscape (sideways, wider than tall).

Copies   Enter the number of copies to be printed.

Cartridges   Identify the font cartridges that are currently installed in your printer. The cartridges you want to use may not be listed. If this is the case, select the Fonts button, select the cartridges, and return to the Cartridges list to make the selection.

Finding Fonts   A *font* is a set of characters that have the same typeface and type size and which can be used with your printer. For example, Courier and Helvetica are two common fonts. Fonts can be stored on cartridges or software form (called soft fonts) in a directory.

Pressing the **F**onts button brings you to a screen where you can install soft fonts or cartridges that are not shown. However, Lotus Corporation recommends that you use the installation program which came with the soft fonts you will use. The **O**ptions button leads to advanced options that are useful to people publishing at a professional level.

When you're done selecting printer setup options, select the OK button to close the dialog box. If you returned to the File Print dialog box, choose OK to print or Cancel to return to Notes without printing.

Changing Page Settings

If the printed result is not what you expected or you want to dress up the outcome, you may want to check the page settings. Select File Page Setup. The dialog box which appears in Figure 8.3 becomes available. As you can see, there are many options at your fingertips.

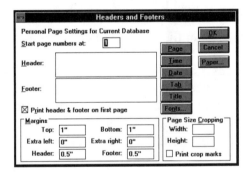

Figure 8.3 The dialog box after selecting Page Setup.

In the Page Setup dialog box, the settings for the current database appear. You can change these settings, but any changes you make are in place until changed again.

You can enter the number of the page on which to start page numbering (**S**tart page numbers at). You can also identify whether headers and footers should print on the first page (**Pr**int header & footer on first page). If this check box is not checked, any headers and footers you enter will print on the second page. Enter text to appear in a **H**eader or **F**ooter. When you enter headers or footers you can select any of these buttons to insert the symbols for the effect described:

Page &P is entered to print the page number on each page.

Time &T is inserted to print the time of the print.

Date &D appears to print the date of the print.

Ta**b** I appears to indicate a tab has been inserted.

Title & W is entered to print the window title (name of docment).

Two other buttons are available on the Page Setup dialog box. Choose Fonts to select a font, size, style, and color. Select Paper to identify the source of paper for the first page and subsequent pages. For example, if your printer accesses two paper sources, you may want to put letterhead in one source and regular paper in the second source.

The Page Setup dialog box also allows you to control Margins. Top and Bottom indicate the amount of white space to place at the top and bottom of the page. Extra left and Extra right identify the amount of extra space to add to the left and right margins beyond the regular document appearance. The Header and Footer margins identify the amount of margin to be included in the header and footer.

Finally, the Page Setup dialog box allows you to set the Page Size Cropping which reduces the size of the print area further.

When you are done with the dialog box, choose OK to close it, and then try printing your document again to see if the changes you made improved your printout.

In this lesson, you learned the steps to print documents, how to change printer settings, and how to change settings that affect how the printed page appears. In the next lesson, you will learn how to format text.

Handling Text, Paragraphs, and Pages

In this lesson, you will learn how to format text, paragraphs, and pages to get the results you want.

Cutting, Copying, and Pasting Text

In Lesson 6, you used the Clipboard to copy entire documents while working in a view. In Lesson 7, you learned how to select text in a document. Now let's combine these skills to cut, copy, and paste text within a document.

To Cut or Copy . . . That Is the Question The lingo can be confusing. *Cutting* removes the text and places it in the Clipboard. *Copying* leaves the text in place and puts a copy of the text in the Clipboard. *Pasting* simply brings the contents of the Clipboard into the document at the location of your insertion point.

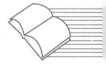

To cut or copy text, follow these steps:

1. Select the text to cut or copy, as you learned in Lesson 7.

2. Choose Edit Cut (or press Ctrl+X) or Edit Copy (or press Ctrl+C). The selected text is placed in the Clipboard.

To paste, follow these steps:

1. Place your insertion point where you want the text to appear.

2. Select Edit Paste (or press Ctrl+V). The text in the Clipboard appears.

Formatting Text

In most fields, you just enter numbers or letters; you don't worry about formatting. However, if your document is a letter or a report, it would be nice to be able to dress up the format. Fortunately, Notes provides a way to do just that, through the use of Rich Text fields.

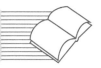

The Richness of Rich Text A *Rich Text* field is designated on a form by the person who designed the form. Rich Text fields allow for styling of color, emphasis, fonts, graphics, and other special characteristics. Only the information in Rich Text fields can be controlled by text formatting.

There are two ways to apply formatting in a Rich Text field:

• Select the text, and then choose the text formats to affect it.

• Apply a text format to affect the text entered after the format is applied.

To do the former, select the text before performing the following steps. To do the latter, simply position the insertion point where you will begin typing after formatting. Then follow these steps:

1. Select Text Font (or press Ctrl+K). The Font dialog box appears (Figure 9.1) with fonts specific with your printer.

2. Select a Font Name & Size. The size is measured in points (one point equals 1/72 of an inch). Select Display to see the fonts available for your display or Printer to select those available for the selected printer.

3. Choose a Color for the text (if you don't want black).

4. Select any combination of attributes: Normal, Bold, Italic, Underline, Strikethrough, Superscript, and Subscript.

5. Select OK when you are done.

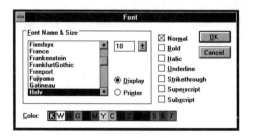

Figure 9.1   Font dialog box.

Several format options are available without going through the Font dialog box. Table 9.1 shows how to choose these options. (Enlarging text increases it to the next available size and reducing text decreases the text to the next available size.)

Table 9.1 Format options.

Format	Menu/Mouse Activity	Keyboard Activity
Normal	Text Normal	Ctrl+T
Bold	Text Bold	Ctrl+B
Italic	Text Italic	Ctrl+I
Underline	Text Underline	Ctrl+U
Enlarge	Text Enlarge	F2
Reduce	Shift+Text Enlarge	Shift+F2

Paragraph Formatting

Paragraph formatting refers to the format features that affect the entire chunk of text, rather than individual letters. It includes margins, tab stops, indents, and alignment.

As with the formatting of text, you must be in Edit mode and you must be in a Rich Text field to format paragraphs. If you select text, paragraph formats are applied to the selected text. If you don't, the formatting affects text from the insertion point on.

Using the Text Paragraph Dialog Box

Many paragraph format options are controlled by selecting Text Paragraph (or pressing Ctrl+J) and using the Text Paragraph dialog box which is shown in Figure 9.2.

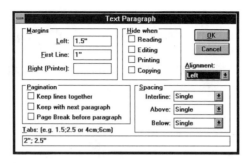

Figure 9.2   The Text Paragraph dialog box.

In the Text Paragraph dialog box, you can enter the Margins.

- The Left margin sets the point at which text begins on the left side of the page.

- The First Line setting allows you to set up hanging indents, bulleted items, or numbered lists. (The numbered steps in this book are examples of the use of hanging indents. The margin for the first line, with the step number, is less than the margin for the step itself.)

- Right (Printer) allows you to set a different margin to be used for printing only. Sometimes text that fits on-screen comfortably enough to read is more attractive printed in a smaller font. In that case, you would want to set the Right (Printer) option to avoid having to change the font each time you want to print the document.

The text Paragraph dialog box also allows you to control how Pagination affects a paragraph.

- Choose Keep lines together to make sure all lines of the paragraph get printed on the same page.

- Choose Keep with next paragraph to keep the preceding paragraph on the same page as the following paragraph.

- Choose Page Break before paragraph to place a page break before the paragraph.

In the Tabs text box, indicate the number of inches or centimeters for each tab stop. (Later in this lesson, you'll learn how to set tab stops from the Ruler.)

The Hide when option on the Text Paragraph dialog box allows you to control what can be seen in your document. You can choose to hide paragraphs when reading, editing, printing, or copying.

You can also control the Alignment of characters. The alignment of text is sometimes referred to as "justification." Text can be aligned in any of these ways:

- Left, which uses a justified left margin and a ragged right margin.

- Right, which has a justified right margin and a ragged left margin.

- Center, which leaves both the left and right margin ragged.

- Full, which inserts spacing as needed for a justified left and right margin.

- None, which prevents text from wrapping around at the end of a line.

Finally, you can determine the Spacing of text, which is the amount of white space between lines. Interline sets spacing for the lines within a paragraph. Above and Below control the spacing before and after the paragraph.

Using the Ruler

Notes has a ruler which many people prefer over the Text Paragraph dialog box for setting tabs and margins. There is a catch: you must have a mouse to use the ruler.

The ruler appears below the SmartIcons (see Figure 9.3). The upper triangle controls the first line of the paragraph. The lower triangle controls the rest of the paragraph. The arrows identify tab stops. In the figure, the lower triangle is set to the right of the upper triangle, creating the hanging indents shown in the body of the text.

To change settings on the ruler, follow these steps:

1. In Edit mode, select View Show Ruler (or press Ctrl+R) if the Ruler is not already visible.

2. Select the paragraphs to affect. For one paragraph, place the insertion point in the paragraph. For multiple paragraphs, select them. For all paragraphs, use Edit, Select All (press Ctrl+A).

3. To set the left margin, move the upper and lower triangles as desired.

4. Click with the mouse to add or remove tab settings.

Indenting and Outdenting Press F7 in the first line to indent that line only. Press F8 to indent the entire paragraph. Press Shift+F7 in the first line to outdent that line only. Press Shift+F8 to outdent the entire paragraph.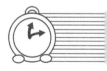

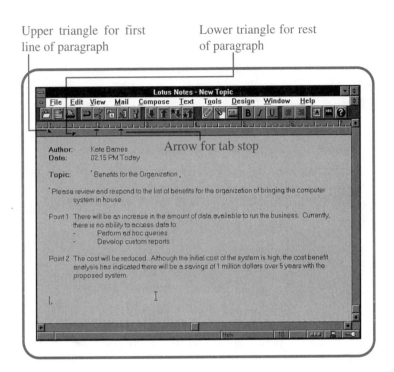

Figure 9.3 The ruler.

Page Formatting

Page breaks appear as solid lines across the page. You can see where pages will break by selecting View Show Page Breaks. A page break can be manually inserted by selecting Edit Insert Page Break (or by pressing Ctrl+L). To get rid of a manually inserted page break, highlight it and press Delete.

Pages can also include headers and footers with titles, page numbers, dates, or any information desired.

Headers and Footers   A *header* appears on the top of the page when printed. A *footer* appears at the bottom.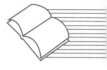

To set a document header or footer, follow these steps:

1. Make sure you are in Edit mode (press Ctrl+E if necessary).

2. Select Edit Header/Footer.

3. In the Edit Header/Footer dialog box, type in the text for the Header and/or Footer.

4. Select any of the following:

   Page   &P is entered to print the page number on each page.

   Time   &T is inserted to print the time of the print.

   Date   &D appears to print the date of the print.

   Tab   I88 appears to indicate a tab has been inserted.

   Title   &W is entered to print the window title (usually the name of the document).

   Fonts   To select a font, size, style, and color.

5. Select OK.

Lesson 10

Find/Replace, Spell, and Tables

In this lesson, you will learn how to find and replace text, spell check a document, and use tables.

Find and Replace

The ability to find and/or replace text within a document can be invaluable. For example, you may need to find specific text in order to locate a topic in a document, or you may need to find and replace text that needs to be changed throughout the document.

To find and replace text, follow these steps:

1. Select Edit Find & Replace (or press Ctrl+F or select the SmartIcon).

2. The Find and Replace dialog box appears. (See Figure 10.1.)

3. Enter the text that you want to find in the Find text box.

4. If you want to replace the specified text, enter the replacement text in the Replace With text box.

5. Select any of these check boxes to further define the search:

Case Sensitive   Exactly matches the case entered (upper-or lowercase).

Accent Sensitive   Matches the accent with the text.

Backward   Searches backward.

Whole Word   Finds whole words only (not partial matches, such as entering "love" as the text to find, and finding "lovely").

6. Select one of the following buttons:

Replace   Replaces the text found (highlighted). This stops the search but you remain in the dialog box to continue using the options.

Cancel   Stops the find operation completely.

Find Next   Begins or continues the find. Once the find has started, you can press Ctrl+G to find the next occurrence.

Replace Then Find   Replaces the text found and finds the next occurrence.

Replace All   Replaces all occurrences of the specified text without stopping at each occurrence. (A warning appears before you can proceed.)

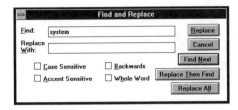

Figure 10.1   The Find and Replace dialog box.

Spell Checking

No work in documents is complete until you've spell-checked the document. You may spell check a word, a portion of the document, or the entire document. The spell checker verifies the words against words in the Notes dictionary. You must be in Edit mode (press Ctrl+E if necessary) to spell check.

To spell check, follow these steps:

1. To spell check a word or a portion of text, select it. Otherwise, go on to the next step.

2. Select Tools Spell Check or select the Tools Check Spelling SmartIcon.

3. When a word is found that does not match a word in the dictionary, the Tools Check Spelling dialog box appears (see Figure 10.2).

4. Choose one of the following buttons:

   Guess   Displays possible spellings in the Guesses text box.

Correct   Replaces the word with the guess you've selected or with changes you've entered in the **E**dit text box.

Accept   Accepts the word as misspelled throughout the rest of the document.

Define   Adds the word to your dictionary so it is not identified as misspelled in the future.

Ignore   Bypasses this occurrence of the misspelling. The next occurrence will be identified.

Done   Ends spell checking.

5. A message appears when the spell check operation is complete.

Figure 10.2   The Tools Check Spelling dialog box.

Expanding the Dictionary

You might get tired of seeing some of the same words marked every time you spell check (such as proper names). To prevent Notes from stopping at commonly used special words, add them to your personal dictionary. You must be in Edit mode when using spell options.

To add a word to the dictionary, follow these steps:

1. Type in the word(s) to add, leaving a space between each word.

2. Select Tools Spell Check.

3. Add the word to the dictionary by selecting Define.

4. Continue spell checking the list.

Using Tables

Notes allows you to add tables in Rich Text fields. (See Lesson 9 for more information on Rich Text fields.) These are the steps to add a table (settings you enter may be changed later):

1. Make sure you are in Edit mode and have the insertion point in a Rich Text field.

2. Choose Edit Insert Table.

3. The Insert Table dialog box appears. (See Figure 10.3.) Enter the Number of rows, the Number of columns, the Left margin, the amount of Space between rows, and the Space between columns. You may set the border around each cell as a Single line, Double (thick) line, or None. Finally, set the Table Width. If you choose Fit to window, the table is resized as the window is resized. If you choose Constant, Notes allows you to enter a fixed table width that does not change.

4. Select OK when you are done.

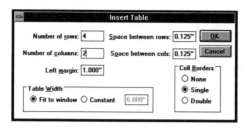

Figure 10.3   The Insert Table dialog box.

Cells   Each rectangular area in a table is referred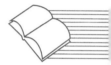
to as a *cell*. Each cell has a column and row number
starting from the upper left corner. The first cell is
column 1, row 1. The cell to the right of that is
column 2, row 1.

Use the mouse or Tab keys to move within a table. To
edit the number of rows and columns in a table, select Edit
Table Insert Row/Column. You may choose to Insert a row
or column. A row will appear above the insertion point, or
a column will appear to the left of the insertion point, or you
may Append a row (to the end) or append a column (to the
right) of the table. Choose Edit Table Delete Row/Column
to delete.

Under the Edit Table command, you also have the
option to change the format of the table. Select Edit Table
Format. Select the row and column of the cell you want to
affect. Then enter the changes. Many of the original settings
can be changed. In addition, you can choose the type of
justification for text in columns or change the border
appearance within a table. You may also control column
width with the ruler.

Lesson 11

Tying Information Together

In this lesson, you will learn to link and attach documents, as well as to annotate text with PopUps.

Linking Documents

Documents can be linked within or across databases. Linked documents can have different views and be on separate servers. To use a linked document, you must have access rights to the documents involved.

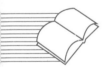

Doclinks Notes calls the linking of documents *doclink.*

Why link documents? Linking documents establishes a cross reference to other information without having to keep multiple copies of the information. For example, you may want to reference a Procedure document in a document you are creating on working with contractors (called Contractors). You could copy the Procedure document into the new Contractors document, but after the information is copied, the Procedure document could become outdated. Creating a doclink from the Contractors document will ensure that the reader always has the current Procedure document readily available, because the doclink will be updated anytime the original Procedure document is. Doclinks are also useful for providing detail that only some of your readers will want to consult.

Using a Doclink

Doclinks are represented by the doclink symbol (see Figure 11.1). To use an existing doclink, double-click on the doclink symbol with the mouse, or press the right arrow key until the doclink symbol is enclosed in a box, and then press the Spacebar. You are taken to the linked document. To return to the original document, press Esc or select the Control Menu box and select Close (or press Ctrl+F4).

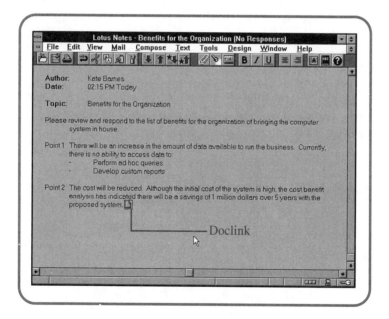

Figure 11.1   A doclink symbol.

The Missing Link   Your selection of a doclink may be unsuccessful. A message may appear saying the document couldn't be located. This can indicate that the document has been deleted, that the view used when the document was linked has been deleted, or that the database is gone. Another type of message you might see is that you have no authorization to open the database. Contact the Notes Administrator if you cannot determine the source of the problem.

Making a Doclink

You can enter as many doclinks in a document as you like. To enter a doclink, follow these steps:

1. Identify the document to be linked to by opening the document or selecting it on a view. (This is the document the reader will go to.)

2. Select Edit Make DocLink. The information is placed in the Clipboard.

3. Open the document in which you want the doclink to appear. (Make sure the document is in Edit mode.)

4. Select Edit Paste. Or press Ctrl+V or select the Edit Paste SmartIcon. The doclink symbol appears.

Think of Others   A common mistake many new users make when adding doclinks is linking to documents to which the reader does not have access. Think about your current (and potential) readers as you create doclinks. Also, consider the probable life of the document to which you are linking in order to make sure that the document will be available to others.

Attaching Documents

You can create an attachment with Notes. (This doesn't refer to an attachment of an emotional nature.) Notes lets you attach a file to a Notes document. A copy of the file is attached to the document and the original file is left untouched.

But Notes Documents Aren't Files You can attach one or more files from other software programs to a Notes document. For example, you may want to attach a Microsoft Word document or a Lotus 1-2-3 file, but because Notes documents aren't files (they are part of a database), you can't attach a Notes document to another document. You must copy the desired information into the document or send the documents together through the Mail options. (See Lesson 12 to learn about Mail.)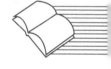

Attachments are handy when you want to send information along with a mail memo or document but not change either document. Also, because you can send nearly any type of non-Notes document, you don't have to change the format of the text. When someone wants to use the attached file, it may be used with the original application. For example, if you attach a Microsoft Word document to a file, the reader would view the Microsoft Word document using Microsoft Word (not Notes).

No Automatic Update   Unlike linked documents, attachments do not update when the original document is updated.

If specified by the database designer, a paper clip symbol appears to the left of the document name in a view (see Figure 11.2). In a document, an icon appears for the type of file along with the file name (see Figure 11.3).

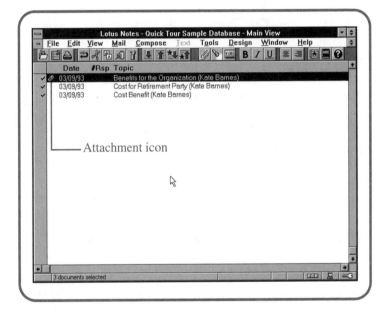

Figure 11.2   The icon for an attachment in a view.

Creating an Attachment

Use these steps to create an attachment:

1. Select Edit Insert File Attachment (or select the Edit Insert Attachment SmartIcon).

2. The Insert Attachment dialog box appears. Identify the file in the File Name text box. Change the Drives and Directories as needed. Deselect the Compress check box if you don't want to compress the file to save space.

3. Select Insert. The icon for the attachment is inserted in your document.

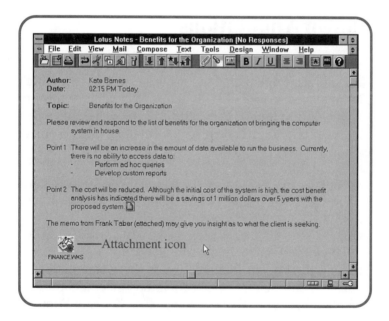

Figure 11.3   The icon for an attachment in a document.

Using an Attachment

To look at the attachment, open the document that contains an attachment. Select the command Edit Attachment. (This command is only available if the open document has an attachment.) Select Information to find out the file name, length, and date last modified. Select Detach to make a separate copy of the attachment file which will not be attached to any document. The file and type you specify is saved in the directory of your choice. Select Launch to start the application under which the file was created (such as Microsoft Word) to view the attachment. If the application is not available, a message will let you know.

PopUp Annotations

Another way to tie information together is to use PopUp Annotations. PopUp annotations are boxes of text which can be placed in Rich Text within a document or form to provide information. They are especially helpful when used in a form to provide prompts about how to complete the form. But they can be used for any information.

PopUps appear in green rectangles. When selected, the text in the PopUp appears. A PopUp is shown in Figure 11.4.

To view a PopUp, make sure you aren't in Edit mode. Click on the PopUp (the area inside the green rectangle) with the mouse. Or use the keyboard by placing the insertion point inside the rectangle and selecting Edit Popup.

To add a PopUp, you must be in Edit mode in a Rich Text field. Follow these steps:

1. Select the text you want to appear in the PopUp green rectangle.

2. Select Edit Insert PopUp.

3. The Insert PopUp dialog box appears. Type in the text that you want to appear in the PopUp. For text, select Text. If you want the result of a formula to appear, select Formula and choose from functions and fields. You can select or deselect the border.

4. Select **OK** when you are done.

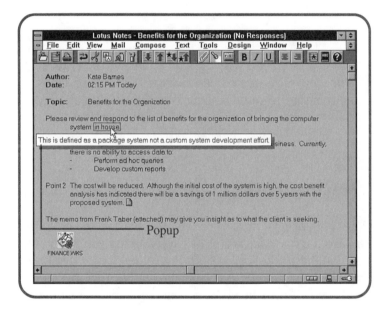

Figure 11.4 A PopUp containing instructions.

Using NotesMail

In this lesson, you will learn how to use NotesMail to send and receive mail messages. (If you are using another mail system, consult materials written for that mail system.)

Viewing Your Mail

Notes is your mail messenger and sorter all rolled into one. To view the mail that Notes has delivered to you, select the mail database like you would any other Notes database. Then select any views to list the mail in the order that works best for you. From the view, you can select mail documents to read.

Handling Addresses

Just like any mail carrier, Notes knows the names and addresses of everyone getting mail. The Name & Address Books hold that information, and you can use them to select destinations for mail you create. The Public Name & Address Book contains information about everyone on the

NotesMail system. Your Personal Name & Address Book is a private list of people you send mail to often.

To view the names in your Personal Name & Address Book, select the Personal Name & Address Book database. Choose View People. To add a person to your Personal Name & Address Book, follow these steps:

1. Select your Personal Name & Address Book database.

2. Choose Compose Person.

3. Complete the information. The First Name may be a nickname. Make sure the Full Name matches the full name in the Public Name & Address Book. Write out addresses with numbers. (For example, enter 2nd Floor as Second Floor.)

4. Once a person has been added, choose File Save (or press Ctrl+S or Esc).

If you regularly send messages to a group of people (like a management team), it is a real timesaver to set the names up as a group. That way, when you send a message, you can select the group. Addressing to everyone is automatically handled. To set up a group:

1. Select the Personal Name & Address Book database.

2. Select Compose Group.

3. Enter a Group Name of your own choosing. Then enter a Description for the group along with the Members names, as shown on the Public Name & Address Book. Separate each name with a comma, semicolon, or hard return.

4. Choose File Save (or press Ctrl+S or Esc).

Composing a Mail Message

The Compose menu is used to create mail. There are several mail forms already defined by Notes. Each may be used to write and send a specific type of mail. This lesson covers how to write and send a memo and how to compose a reply to all the people on an existing memo. The techniques used for these common activities can be used to complete all the other types of forms. The forms include:

- **M**emo to write and send a standard mail memo.

- **M**emo to Manager to write and send a memo to the manager of the database which is active.

- **P**hone Message to write and send a telephone message.

- **R**eply to write and send a reply to a mail message that is selected in a view or is open (as a document).

- Reply To **A**ll to write and send a reply to a message that is selected in a view or is open. Each person listed in the To: and cc: (carbon copy) fields receives a reply. If people are listed in the bcc: (blind carbon copy) field, they receive a reply only if you received the mail originally as a bcc.

To create a NotesMail memo, follow these steps:

1. Choose Compose Memo from the mail menu.

2. The New Memo form shown in Figure 12.1 appears. Complete the address, body, and delivery and storage information in the window. (See the rest of this section for details about filling in the form.)

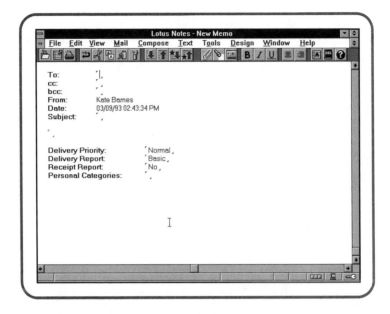

Figure 12.1 The New Memo form.

In the To:, cc:, and bcc: fields in the New Memo form, enter either the first name or the last name if the name is unique in your Personal Name & Address Book, or type in the first and last names or a group name as shown in any Name & Address Book. If you enter more than one name, separate them with commas. Names in the bcc: field are hidden. A bcc recipient will only see his or her own name (not the names of others receiving a bcc). If you enter a name that Notes can't match or a name for which Notes finds more than one match, Notes will send you a message including names from which you may pick.

Using a Name & Address Book is a quick way to complete the To:, cc:, and bcc: fields. From the memo form, select **M**ail **A**ddress to access the Mail Address dialog box shown in Figure 12.2. In this dialog box, select the Address field to complete from the drop-down list. Select the Name & Address Book to use. In the Name area, double-click on the name for the address field, or highlight it and select the Add button. The name appears in the message. Continue selecting names until the address for the message is complete.

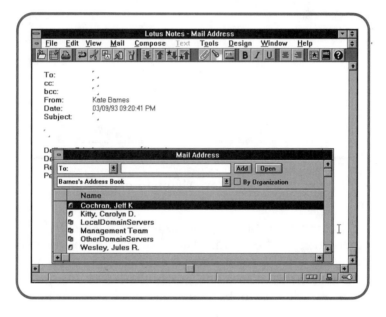

Figure 12.2 The Mail Address dialog box.

Once the address is entered, you can enter a Subject followed by the body of the memo.

The New Memo window also includes the Delivery Priority, Delivery Report, and Receipt Report. Each has preset selections. Place your pointer in the field and press the Spacebar to see the options. The Delivery Priority may be set to High, Low, or Normal and only affects mail being sent off the LAN (Local Area Network). The Delivery

Report may be set to Basic to notify you only if the mail could not be delivered, Confirmed to notify you when the mail is or is not delivered, or No Report to receive no notification. Set the Receipt Report to Yes to be notified when the recipient opens the message or No to avoid such notification.

Finally, on the New Memo window you can enter Personal Categories to categorize the message when saved. This makes it easier to find messages at a later date. Enter commas to separate categories if you enter more than one.

Saving a Message

Once you have composed a message, you may save it with or without sending it. To save a message, select File Save (or press Ctrl+S). Or you can select the File Save SmartIcon.

If you close the message window using File Close Window (or by pressing Ctrl+W) without sending the message first, the Document Save dialog box shown in Figure 12.3 appears. In the dialog box, you may check the Save check box. (The other options on this dialog box are covered in the next section.) If you have already sent the message, you'll be given the typical Notes save option for a document.

Figure 12.3   The Document Save dialog box.

Send a Message

Once a message has been created, you may send it. As you may have guessed in the last section, one way to send a memo is to select File Close Window or press Ctrl+W. On the Document Save dialog box (Figure 12.3) check Save and/or Send the message. Check Sign to add an electronic "signature" from your User ID to the message. Check Encrypt to encrypt the message. Encrypting is a way to control who can read the message. Lesson 14 describes encryption in greater detail.

Another way to send mail is to choose Mail Send. On the Mail Send dialog box, you can check Sign and/or Encrypt and then select the Send button.

 **Attaching Documents**   You can save time by attaching a document to a memo rather than including all the information in the memo. To attach a document to a NotesMail memo in a Rich Text field, select Edit Insert File Attachment. (See Lesson 11 for additional details about attaching files.)

Respond to a Memo

To respond to a memo that has been mailed to you, follow these steps:

1. Select the memo in the view or open the memo.

2. Select Compose Reply (to respond to the sender) or Reply/Reply to All (to reply to all who received the mail. Bcc recipients only get the reply if they received the memo as a bcc.)

3. The New Reply window appears with the appropriate addresses and subject entered. Complete the reply, then send it using Mail Send.

Forwarding Mail

You may need to forward mail to someone else. Perhaps you got the wrong mail or you want to share the information with one or more people. From the view, select or open the memo. Select Mail Forward. Complete the address as usual. The body of the memo is identical to the memo you chose to forward and may be edited. Once the memo is ready to go, send it off.

Setup Options

Select Tools Setup Mail Setup to control setup options. In the Mail Setup dialog box, you can select from the following options:

- Use the radio buttons to identify whether your mail is stored on the server (Server-based mail) or on your workstation (Workstation-based mail).

- Use the check boxes to identify whether you always want to Save Sent Mail, Sign Sent Mail, Encrypt Sent Mail, Encrypt Saved Mail, and/or Check for New Mail Every XX Minutes. If you selected Check for New Mail, you can indicate how often Notes should check for new mail.

Lesson 13

Customizing Notes and Handling Unread Marks

In this lesson, you will learn how to customize the appearance and performance of Notes as well as the specifics about handling documents that have or have not been read.

Customizing

You can customize the physical appearance of Notes on your workstation through the User Setup dialog box. This dialog box also gives you control over other options, such as Startup options. Follow these steps:

1. Select Tools Setup User Setup.

2. The User Setup dialog box appears (see Figure 13.1).

3. Change the settings (a description of each follows).

4. Select OK.

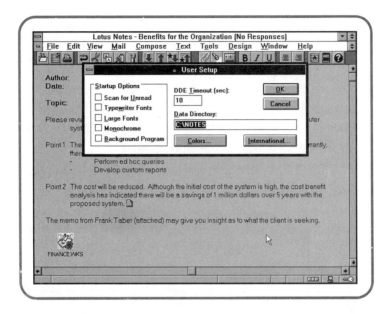

Figure 13.1   The User Setup dialog box.

In the User Setup dialog box, you can control Startup Options. Select from these options:

Scan for Unread   The databases you specify will be checked for unread documents when you start Notes. (Specify the databases in the Scan Unread Preferred Setup dialog box discussed later in this lesson.)

Typewriter Fonts   All documents, views, and database titles will be displayed in monospace fonts rather than proportional fonts (see Figure 13.2). Some users like monospaced fonts because they feel it is easier to control tabs, align columns, and see incorrectly entered spaces. The down side is that typewriter fonts do not display text enhancements (such as bold). Further, you can't use the Text Enlarge command.

Large Fonts   The proportional fonts (the default) are displayed larger and slightly darker. (Compare the text in the background of Figure 13.1 to the large font shown in Figure 13.3.)

Monochrome   On a color monitor, the background is displayed as white, and all the colors are displayed as shades of gray. There is no change in the displays of monochrome monitors.

Background Program   A background program is run on startup. Your Notes Administrator can help set up background programs that should be run.

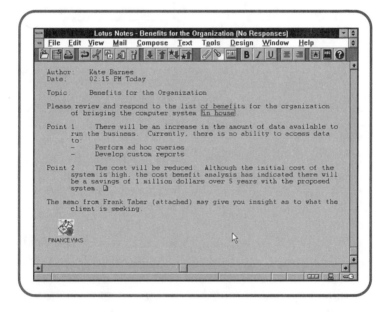

Figure 13.2   Typewriter Font appearance of the workspace.

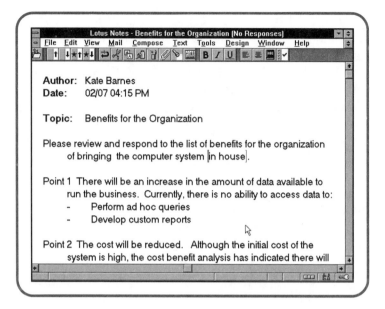

Figure 13.3   Large Font appearance of the workspace.

Also in the User Setup dialog box, you can change the DDE **T**imeout (sec) option to control how many seconds you want Notes to try to establish a link before giving up. (DDE links are covered in Lesson 17.) The **D**ata Directory area of this dialog box tells you where local databases are stored.

Do you not like the colors on your display? On the User Setup dialog box, select the Colors button to change them. The Color Setup dialog box appears, allowing you to select colors for background, text, icons, and imported pictures. To change a color, select the color and slide the mixing bars to change the proportion of color mix. Watch the color you selected to see the result of moving the mixing bar. If you change a color and don't like it, select the Default button on the Color Setup dialog box to return to the original setting.

103

The final option on the User Setup dialog box is the International button, which accesses the International Setup dialog box. In the International Setup dialog box, you can choose between Imperial (inches) or Metric (centimeters) measurement. You select how documents are sorted in a view through the Collation/Casing option. Scandinavian Collation sorts accented characters last; Numbers Last Collation sorts numbers after letters; and French Casing drops accent marks on most letters when they are changed from lower- to uppercase. Select the File Translation button to identify the type of translation when you import non-Notes files. Choose the Dictionary button to change the dictionary used during spell checking.

Nothing Happened   After you change any Startup Options, you must restart Notes for the changes to take effect.

Unread Documents

When you select a document in a view and press Enter or when you click on a document in a view, the document is opened. Notes identifies unopened documents (those you haven't looked at) as *unread*. Identifying unread documents can be a big timesaver. Look for a star or other designation to identify unread documents in views. (Or you may select View Show Unread to display only unread documents.) Once you are in a document, you can press F4 to go to the next unread document or Shift+F4 to go the previous unread document. But how do you find all the unread documents in all the databases of interest?

Automatic Database Scanning

As mentioned earlier in this lesson, when you start Notes, databases you specify (called *preferred databases*) can be automatically scanned for unread documents. This is accomplished by choosing Tools Setup User Setup and checking Scan for Unread. When you start Notes, a dialog box appears for each preferred database with the database name and a count of the unread documents. There are also buttons to mark all documents as read, to look at the next database with unread documents, or to look at the information for the next preferred database.

To identify the preferred databases to be scanned, follow these steps:

1. Select Tools Scan Unread Choose Preferred.

2. The Scan Unread Preferred Setup dialog box appears. This dialog box lists each database on your workspace under Databases to scan. Select each database you want scanned automatically. (If you accidentally highlight a database you don't want scanned, select it again to remove the highlight.)

3. Check the Start Scanner at Notes startup box to begin scanning when Notes is started. (This has the same effect as choosing Tools Setup User Setup and checking Scan for Unread.)

4. Select OK.

If you want to scan the preferred databases at your command (instead of automatically upon startup), select Tools, Scan Unread, Preferred Databases.

Selection   If no selections are made, all databases will be scanned. If you want to "unselect" a preferred database, just select the highlighted database again to deselect it.

We've just looked at scanning for unread documents in preferred databases. You may occasionally want to perform a one-time scan of selected databases. To do this, select the databases in your workspace. Then select Tools Scan Unread Selected Databases.

Controlling Unread Marks

As mentioned, an *unread* document is one that has not been opened. The unread mark is usually a star, but it might be identified in a color or by another indicator. Notes' feature of automatically marking unread documents is all very handy, but Notes has no way of knowing whether you have finished reading a document. In that case, you have to restore the unread star mark. To do that, select the document and choose Tools Unread Marks Mark Selected Unread. You can also mark selected documents as read, if you don't want to keep them for later reading. Just select Tools Unread Marks Mark Selected Read.

Deselecting   When you select documents for any operation (whether to mark as read, to mark as unread, or to print) you'll want to deselect them when the operation is complete. This prevents documents being incorrectly included in future selection activities. To deselect all documents in one operation, choose Edit Deselect All.

Lesson 14
Security

In this lesson, you will learn how to secure documents for confidentiality and how to protect your User ID.

Encryption

You don't need secret agent training to keep information confidential with Notes. Notes allows you to encrypt fields in a document and then choose who you want to be able to read the fields.

Encryption When you *encrypt* the fields in a document, you are simply applying a secret key to the fields. Then you can supply the *encryption key* to anyone you want to be able to look at the document.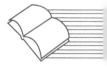

Encryption has many uses, but it is especially helpful in protecting confidential information such as salaries, bids, client names, and contract award amounts. Only users with the encryption key can read encrypted fields. Other users with access to the document but not the encryption key can see all information except the encrypted fields.

Creating an Encryption Key

To create an encryption key, follow these steps:

1. Choose Tools User ID Encryption Keys.

2. Enter your password in the Enter Password dialog box and select OK.

3. The User ID Encryption Keys dialog box appears (see Figure 14.1).

4. Select the New button.

5. In the Add Encryption Key dialog box, enter the Encryption Key Name. Select North American only or International depending on where the encryption key will be used. If desired, enter a Comment regarding the use of the key.

6. Select OK as necessary to return to the workspace.

Figure 14.1   The User ID Encryption Keys dialog box.

Encrypting Document Fields

Before you can encrypt fields, the fields must have been identified as encryptable fields by the former designer. When you work in a document, encryptable fields are designated by red brackets.

There are some rules regarding applying encryption keys to a document. You can apply more than one encryption key to a document. Then users with one or more of the encryption keys can read the encrypted fields in the document. You cannot apply different encryption keys to different fields within a document.

To encrypt the fields in a document, follow these steps:

1. Open the document with the fields to encrypt.

2. Select Edit Security Encryption Keys.

3. The Encryption Keys dialog box appears showing the Encryption **K**eys Available (those you've created) and any Document **E**ncryption Keys (those applied to the document already, if any).

4. Select one or more encryption key, click on Add, and choose OK.

Deactivating Encryption

If you decide to remove the encryption on a document, open the document. Choose Edit Security Encryption Keys. To remove a single encryption key, select it in the Document **E**ncryption Keys area and select Remove. To remove all encryption keys from a document, select the Remove All button.

Controlling Encryption of Many Documents

You can work from a view to add or delete document encryption. These are the steps:

1. Select the documents in the view.

2. Select Edit Security Encryption Keys.

3. The Encryption Keys dialog box appears. Select the Show All button. All the keys used in the selected documents appear in the Document's Encryption Keys area.

4. Select a key then select Add or Remove to effect all documents. Continue until all changes are made.

5. Select OK.

Words of Caution   Never select Show All and then **OK** to leave the dialog box unless you intend for all selected documents to be encrypted with the keys shown. Likewise, if you fail to select Show All and then leave the dialog box by selecting **OK**, all the encryption keys are deleted. Be careful.

Letting Others Know

Encrypted fields in documents are not useful unless the intended audience has the encryption key to see the fields. You can notify a user of the encryption key via NotesMail or by sending them the information outside NotesMail.

If the users are on NotesMail, these are the steps:

1. Select **Mail Send User ID Encryption Key**.

2. Enter your password and select **OK**.

3. The Mail Encryption Key dialog box appears (see Figure 14.2). Select the keys you want to send from the **Encryption Key List**. This is where **Comments** are especially handy. For example, you may enter a description of the documents to which the keys were applied.

4. Select **Mail**.

5. The Mail Address Encryption Key dialog box appears. Enter the **To** and **CC** names of the recipients. (Select **Address** for address book information.) Check **Sign** and **Encrypt** for maximum security.

6. Select **Send**.

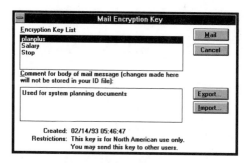

Figure 14.2   Mail Encryption Key dialog box.

If your readers are not NotesMail users, you can export the key to a file server or floppy diskette by performing the following steps:

1. Select Tools User ID Encryption Keys.

2. Enter your password and select OK.

3. The User ID Encryption Keys dialog box appears. Select the keys you want to send from the Encryption Key List and add any Comments about the documents to which the keys are applied.

4. Select Export.

5. The User ID Encryption Key Export dialog box appears. You should enter a Password for maximum security.

6. The Specify File for the Exported Key dialog box appears. Enter the location in which you want to store the encryption key and the name of the file. Select OK when you have created the file.

7. Tell the user where the exported encryption key is stored (and the password if one is set).

Your User ID and Password

The size, number, and uses of Notes' databases make them very valuable to any organization. For that reason, the security set up through the assignment of your User ID and password is no joke. You would not want anyone to access the database and change or delete sensitive data posing as you. To avoid such problems, follow these rules:

- Keep your User ID on a floppy diskette to be inserted in your computer's drive when using Notes. This way, you can lock the diskette in a drawer when not in use. In addition, your User ID file is not available on the server or hard disk for others to access.

- Keep one or more backup copies of your User ID on floppy diskettes in secured locations. It is a good idea to keep one off site in case of theft, fire, or water damage.

- Always password-protect your User ID. (The steps for setting a password appear later in the lesson.)

- Always log off the server when you are done working by pressing F5. Don't start Notes then leave your workstation unattended for long periods of time. That's asking for trouble.

- Change your password periodically, use a password that would be difficult to guess, and DON'T FORGET YOUR PASSWORD. (Write the password down in a very secure place, if necessary.)

You can set or change passwords with these steps:

1. Choose Tools User ID Password Set.

2. Enter your current password (if any) and select OK.

3. You'll go to the Enter Password dialog box. Enter a new password of 31 characters or less and select OK.

4. Enter the password again and select OK.

The password doesn't appear on-screen when entered just in case someone is looking over your shoulder. Also watch who's watching your fingers. Passwords have fallen into the wrong hands by jokers who make a habit of watching hands. Also be careful when you enter a new password. They are case-sensitive; "Icog" is different from "icog."

For additional protection, limit the amount of time your workstation can be left unattended. In the Enter Password dialog box, enter a number of minutes in the **A**utomatically logoff after xx minutes of activity box. This way, if you are called away from your workstation and delayed, Notes will automatically log you off after the time indicated.

Passwords can also be cleared (deleted). To clear a password, choose Tools User **ID** Password Clear.

I Can't Change   It is possible that your password is not set up to be cleared. If you run into trouble trying to clear it, contact your Notes Administrator for more information.

No Local Protection   Passwords don't protect local databases (those stored off the server on a workstation's hard disk). If you work out of the office and have databases stored on a dial-up workstation, make sure no one has access to the workstation.

In this lesson, you learned how to use encryption keys to secure fields in documents and how to secure your User ID and password. In the next lesson, you'll learn how to cut some corners with SmartIcons.

Lesson 15
SmartIcons

In this lesson, you will learn how to streamline keypresses by accessing and using Notes one hundred and ten SmartIcons.

Using SmartIcons

SmartIcons appear below the menu bar in Notes for Windows. Using a SmartIcon is a quick way to execute Notes commands. Just click on a SmartIcon to perform an action. To see what action a SmartIcon performs, point at it and hold down the right mouse button. A description of the SmartIcon appears in the title bar.

Notes has over one hundred predefined SmartIcons. To see them, select Tools SmartIcons. The SmartIcons dialog box shown in Figure 15.1 appears.

To see every SmartIcon available in Notes, scroll through the Available icons box on the left side of the dialog box. Each SmartIcon is followed by a description of the commands that it executes arranged in alphabetical order.

Selected set   SmartIcons in selected set

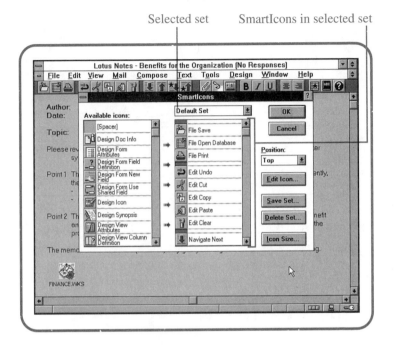

Figure 15.1 The SmartIcons dialog box.

SmartIcons can be selected and placed in sets. For example, in Figure 15.1, the Default Set is the selected set. The SmartIcons under the selected set are those for the default set in the order in which they appear, starting with the File Save SmartIcon. The dialog box also shows the **P**osition for the default set, which is near the top of the workspace.

To select a set, select Tools SmartIcons and select the set you want in the **P**osition desired. Then choose OK. The set appears in your workspace.

Another Set? No, you can't have more than one
SmartIcon set on your workspace at a time. If you
want more SmartIcons to appear, just add them to
the existing set. Editing existing sets is covered later
in this lesson.

Creating Sets

The SmartIcon dialog box is your palette for creating your
own SmartIcon sets. With it, you can select the SmartIcons
you want, in the order you want, with the spacing you want,
and specify the position. This way, you can call up a set at
any time.

Before you create a set, consider what sets you might
find useful. For example, you might want a set to include the
SmartIcons you'll use to control databases from the
workspace. Another SmartIcon set may be developed for
handling tables if you use them often. And another set might
be put together for NotesMail commands.

To create a set, follow these steps:

1. Select Tools SmartIcons and select the existing
   SmartIcon set that is closest to what you want to create.

2. Drag a copy of any SmartIcon you want from the left
   Available icons box to the box on the right. Use Spacer
   to insert spaces. Drag the SmartIcons to place them in
   the order you want them. Then drag any SmartIcons that
   you don't want out of the box.

3. Select the **P**osition (Left, Top, Right, or Bottom of the workspace or Floating for a floating box). Figure 15.2 shows a floating box.

4. Select **S**ave Set.

5. In the Save SmartIcon Set dialog box, enter the **N**ame of the SmartIcon set (up to 15 characters). Then enter a **F**ile name (up to 8 characters) followed by .SMI and select OK.

Floating SmartIcon box

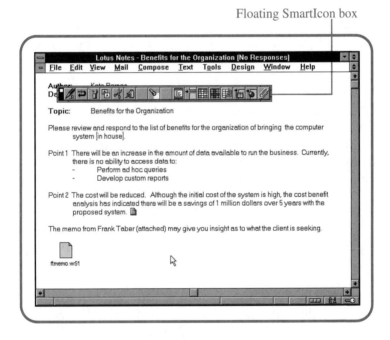

Figure 15.2 A floating SmartIcon box.

Using the Float Floating SmartIcon boxes can be dragged anywhere on the workspace. If you find that the top, bottom, left, and right positions take up too much space, use the float.

Draw a Blank   If you will create numerous sets of SmartIcons, you might want a "blank set" to use in creating new sets. By doing so, you'll avoid having to drag SmartIcons that you don't want out of the new set. To create a blank set, follow all the steps to create any set. Drag all the SmartIcons out of an existing set and name the new set "blank." Use it as the basis for new sets.

Editing, Sizing, and Deleting Sets

To edit an existing SmartIcon set, use essentially the same procedure as you did to create a new set. Choose Tools SmartIcons and select the set. Then add, delete, or rearrange SmartIcons by dragging, and set a new Position if you like. Select OK.

You can control the size of SmartIcons. Select Tools SmartIcons Icon Size. Select the size and then select OK. You may want to experiment to see what size is best on your workstation.

To delete a set, choose Tools SmartIcons Delete Set. Select the set to delete and choose OK.

In this lesson, you learned how to use SmartIcons and control SmartIcon sets. In the next lesson, you'll learn how to import and export information in Notes.

Lesson 16

Importing and Exporting Information

In this lesson, you will learn how to import and export information to and from Notes.

Why Import and Export?

Importing and exporting has little to do with international trade and everything to do with accessing the right information available in the right format.

 Import and Export   When you *import* information, you get information from a source outside of Notes, bring that information into Notes, and include it in Notes views, documents, or forms. Exporting is just the opposite. When you *export*, you take information from a Notes document and place it in a format that another program can use.

Why import and export? Let's look at importing first.

In Lesson 11, you learned that complete files from other sources (such as Microsoft Word) can be attached to a Notes document. This allows your reader to refer to the

120

attached document through the original program. For example, attach a Microsoft Word document to a Notes document, and another user will be able to view the information using Microsoft Word. With importing, the need for using another program to view the information is eliminated. Instead, the Microsoft Word text would be brought into Notes. Then you can edit the imported information as you like. (If you are using a Windows application, you may want to copy and paste using the Clipboard instead of using Import/Export.)

Exporting is necessary to get Notes information to someone who does not have access to Notes. It is also handy if you want to manipulate Notes information using other programs. For example, you may want to take raw data from Notes, export it to a Lotus 1-2-3 spreadsheet, then perform the sophisticated calculations and sorting that is available in Lotus 1-2-3.

How to Import

You can import popular word processing, spreadsheet, and graphics files (including scanned images) into Notes. You can also import the ASCII files (which are common personal computer file formats).

Before getting on with the steps to import, there are a few tips for spreadsheet and graphic imports. When you import spreadsheet data into a view, each row of the spreadsheet becomes a document and each column is a field in a document. When you import spreadsheet data into a document, all the imported information is placed in the document. Graphics can be imported into a document or into the Rich Text field of a form after selecting Compose and the form.

Avoiding Surprises Sometimes, an import doesn't yield the result you expected. Always save a copy of the information you are importing in case you want to "lose" the results of the import and return to the original information. The file you are importing is not affected by the import.

To import information, follow these steps:

1. Open the view or document (or for a graphic image, open a document or form) to import into. Information can only be imported into a Rich Text field.

2. Select File Import. (If the Import option is grayed, make sure you are in Edit mode.)

3. The Import dialog box shown in Figure 16.1 appears. Select the file type from the List Files of Type drop-down list. (The list reflects the type of files under the selected drive and directory. Change Directories and Drives as necessary.) Identify the file to import by selecting File Name. (Only files that correspond to the file type appear in the File Name text box.)

4. Click on the Import button.

5. If you are importing an ASCII file into a document, you will identify whether or not you want to preserve existing line breaks. If you are importing an ASCII file into a view or a spreadsheet file into a view or document, other dialog boxes (described later) will appear. Provide the necessary information and select OK.

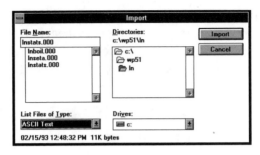

Figure 16.1   The Import dialog box.

Structured Text Import Dialog Box

The Structured Text Import dialog box shown in Figure 16.2 appears when you want to import a document into a view. Select a form under Use Form. Identify whether you want the Inter-Document Delimiter to be Form Feed (the Return symbol) or an ASCII Character Code that you identify. Generally, you'll stick with the form feed. Identify whether you want to Import as a Main Document(s) or a Response Document(s). For body text, identify if you want to Justify text (to wrap the text to fit in a Notes window) or to Preserve Line Breaks (to keep existing line breaks).

Worksheet Import Dialog Box

When you import a spreadsheet into a document, the Worksheet Import dialog box appears (see Figure 16.3). You can import the Entire Worksheet or just the Named

123

Range. If you choose the latter, enter the **R**ange Name in the text box. If you are importing a spreadsheet into a view, you might also have to identify the form, whether to import as a response or main document, and how to define columns.

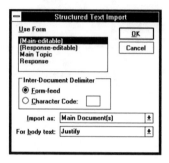

Figure 16.2 The Structured Text Import dialog box.

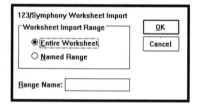

Figure 16.3 Worksheet Import dialog box.

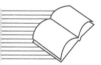

Format File Defined You can define *Column Format Descriptor Files* (COL File) containing import translation information for spreadsheets or ASCII text. See your Notes documentation for more information about Column Format Descriptor Files.

Other Dialog Boxes

Other dialog boxes may appear, depending on the type of import you are performing. For example, there are special dialog boxes for importing Agenda STF files, tabular ASCII files, and graphics files. Most dialog boxes request some of the fields just defined. Some require additional information. Consult Notes Help if a dialog box appears specific to the type of file you are importing.

How to Export

Notes documents or views can be exported into a format compatible for another program to use.

To export, follow these steps:

1. Open a document or view and select information to export.

2. Choose File Export.

3. The Export dialog box (shown in Figure 16.4) appears. Identify the type of file format you want to export to under List Files of Type. Identify the File Name (along with the drive and directory).

4. Click on the Export button.

5. If you are exporting ASCII text, you can change the number of characters in a line. Other dialog boxes appear, depending on the type of export you're performing. These are described later. Provide the requested information and select OK.

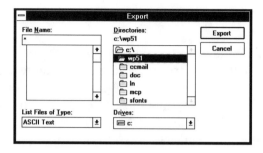

Figure 16.4   The Export dialog box.

Dialog Boxes

Special dialog boxes appear if you are exporting a view to
a spreadsheet or to a tabular ASCII file. (Note: You cannot
export a document to a spreadsheet file.) Under Document
Selection, choose whether you want to export **S**elected
Documents or **A**ll Documents. You can also choose **I**n-
clude View Titles to include the view's columns names in
the export.

If you choose to export one or more documents from a
view as structured text, the Structured Text Export dialog
box will appear. Indicate whether you want the Inter-
Document Delimiter to be **F**orm Feed (the Return symbol)
or a **C**haracter Code. Choose whether you want to **E**xport
All documents in view or only the Selected documents in
the view. Finally, enter a value for the option **W**rap words
at xx characters per line, which indicates the number of
characters you want in a line before that line wraps around
to a new one.

Linking and Embedding Information

In this lesson, you will learn how to link and embed text from other applications.

Why Link or Embed Information?

Linking and embedding allows you to access information from non-Notes applications in a Notes document, and then to activate the original application for editing. In addition, the information in a link is updated when the original file is updated. The information linked or embedded is often referred to as an *object*.

Suppose you have Lotus 1-2-3 spreadsheet information that you want to bring into a Notes document. If you embed the information, you can update the information with Lotus 1-2-3 while it remains in the Notes document. When you do so, the update does not affect the original 1-2-3 file. Choose embed if you want to make the information available for further updating in Lotus 1-2-3 from Notes while not affecting the original file. If you link the information, you can update the Notes document to reflect the latest and greatest changes in the Lotus 1-2-3 file. (You would want to import the file if you thought Lotus 1-2-3 would not be available to you or other future editors of the Notes document.) This is especially important to consider if you are linking or embedding a file on your local hard disk which is not available to others.

DDE and OLE You can use *DDE (Dynamic Data Exchange)* to create links. You can use *OLE (Object Linking and Embedding)* to link or embed objects. In addition, with OLE you can use another application from within Notes to create objects for a Notes document. This lesson covers both DDE and OLE. Several Lotus and Microsoft products (as well as other products) support DDE and OLE. If you are unsure whether an application you use supports DDE or OLE, consult the documentation for the application or check with your Notes Administrator.

How to Link or Embed

The easiest way to link or embed is to copy the object to the Clipboard and then paste it into the Notes document with Paste Special.

Don't Move When you create a link, the source file cannot be moved or deleted. Otherwise, the linked document cannot find the object required for the link unless you change the link.

Follow these steps to create a link or to embed an object:

1. From the original application, make sure the file is saved. Then copy the object you want to include in Notes to the Clipboard (usually with the Edit Copy command).

2. Open the Notes document (make sure you are in Edit mode) and place the insertion point in a Rich Text field.

3. Select Edit Paste Special.

4. The Paste Special dialog box appears (see Figure 17.1). Select the data format in the Display As list. Then select Paste to copy the object from the Clipboard (and not allow it to be edited in the future through the application), Link to link to the original file for updating later and editing through the source application, or Embed to allow for later editing using the source application.

Figure 17.1   The Paste Special dialog box.

You can control how long Notes attempts to complete a DDE link. Select Tools Setup User Setup. In the DDE Timeout (sec) text box, enter the amount of time to try to establish a link before stopping. The default is 10 seconds. If you routinely run out of time before a link is established, you might want to try extending the time.

Can't Link or Embed   The Link and Embed options on the Paste Special dialog box may be dimmed and unavailable. If so, the application you're using might require that you save the original file before copying the object to the Clipboard. If you did not do that, the file location wasn't

copied, and Notes can't locate the appropriate application. Or the options might be unavailable because your application does not support DDE or OLE.

Embedding OLE Objects

Another means of embedding an entire file as an OLE object also allows you to create an object. These are the steps to embed a file:

1. From a Rich Text field in a Notes document, select Edit Insert Object.

2. In the Insert Object dialog box, select the Object Type then Choose File.

3. In the Insert Object Choose File dialog box, select the File Name (change the drive, directory, and file type if necessary).

4. Choose OK to return to the Insert Object dialog box.

5. Select Display Format. On the Insert Object Display Format dialog box, select the format and then OK as required to return to your Notes document. The file is embedded.

To create an object, select Edit Insert Object. Choose the Object Type and select OK. You are taken to the application you selected to create the object. Create the object. Then use the File Update command in the application to complete the object. (Or exit and respond Yes to the message asking if you want to update the Notes document.) You can then exit the application.

Updating and Changing a Link

Links can be updated automatically when the Notes document is accessed, or you can update them manually by selecting View Refresh Fields (or by pressing F9).

You can make changes in existing links, such as changing the object, or manually updating, unlinking, or changing the characteristics of the link. To make changes, select Edit Links. The Edit Links dialog box is shown in Figure 17.2. On it, select the link in the Links list. Choose the button according to the change required. These are your options:

- Activate   Launches the application and opens the file. Before you can activate a DDE link, the application must be running, and the linked file must be open. If you linked part of a file, the whole file might appear even though only the linked part will be updated. Once you have edited the information, it is automatically updated if the link is set up for automatic updating. If it is not, select Update from the Edit Links dialog box or select View Refresh Fields (or press F9).

- Update   Manually updates a link or updates an inactive automatic link.

- Unlink   Removes the link from the Notes document. If you choose Unlink and then change your mind, you can choose Unlink again before leaving the Edit Links dialog box to restore the link. Once a link is unlinked and this dialog box is closed, the linking steps must be performed again to reestablish the link.

- Deactivate   Terminates the activated link after editing. You must deactivate an activated link before you can change the link using the Change Link button.

• **C**hange Link   Takes you to the Change Link dialog box (see Figure 17.3). In this dialog box, you can change the name of the **A**pplication used to create the linked data, the path and/or file name in the **T**opic text area, the **I**tem linked (such as a spreadsheet range), or the **U**pdate Type (Automati**c** or **M**anual).

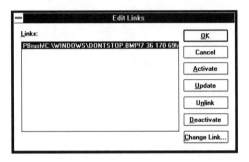

Figure 17.2   The Edit Links dialog box.

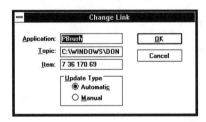

Figure 17.3   The Change Link dialog box.

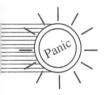

It's an Icon   Usually, the contents of the linked or embedded object will appear in the Notes document. However, if the object contains several data formats, an icon may appear. If so, double-click on the icon or select Edit *[type of object]* or Edit Links to edit the object.

Lesson 18
Working Out
of the Office

In this lesson, you will learn how to work out of the office and access Notes databases.

Working Remotely

With Notes, you can physically leave the office, but not leave the office completely behind. Or you can work at an office where there is no Notes server, yet tie into the server at another site.

Usually, workstations are attached to the server via cables. When you work away from the server, you are working *remotely*. You will contact the server over telephone lines using a modem, which is referred to as working as a *dial-up workstation*. You keep the telephone connection while you work, which makes it possible for you to use the databases on the server. This is called working *interactively*, because the work you do immediately updates the databases on the server. Or you could create a *replica database* (a copy) on your computer's hard disk and then *replicate* (exchange) data from the server's shared databases to your replica. This would allow you to work *locally* (without connection to the server).

Setting Up the Dial-Up Workstation

Before you can function as a dial-up workstation, you must have Notes installed on your workstation, and you must have a modem that will work with Notes. In addition, setup options need to be verified.

Your Notes Administrator may have completed the setup activities described in this section. If not, you will need to know the name and phone number of the server you wish to contact, your modem port, and any special modem settings. If you feel you do not have the technical knowledge to complete the setup options, contact the Notes Administrator for help.

Choose Tools Setup Network Ports to make sure the port for the telephone connection is correct. An asterisk before the port in the Port List indicates which port is enabled.

- To enable a different port, select the port and make sure the Enable Port box is checked.

- To change the ports which appear in the Port List, select Add Port or Delete Port and complete the information required.

- To change the port information, select Redefine Port.

- To change modem settings, select Additional Setup. Complete the settings to reflect your port and modem.

To identify the server, select Tools Setup Location Setup and complete the details about the server to which you'll connect.

- Select Server-based mail if your mail database is on the server. Select Workstation-based mail if your mail database is local (stored on your remote computer's hard disk).

- Enter the name of the Home Server and the Time Zone.

- If you use a credit card or other number before dialing the phone number for the server, you may enter that number in the Phone Dialing Prefix text box.

- If you intend to change these settings often, you might want to check Do Location Setup every time Notes is started for a reminder to change the settings.

Because you will be working dial-up, select Tools Setup Notes Setup and make sure Dial-up Workstation is selected. Complete other options as required.

If you are using NotesMail, check out Tools Setup Mail Setup and specify Server-based mail or Workstation-based mail. Check the other options. If you will use replica databases select the Replication button. A dialog box appears in which you control how local changes to documents affect the server and how much data winds up stored on your workstation.

- Select Do not copy local changes or deletions back to server if you want to delete documents from your local replica databases and don't want those deletions to affect server databases.

- Select Copy from server only first part (~40KB) of large documents and copy from server no attachments to limit what is copied from the server to your local workstation. Approximately the first 80 pages of a document (and no attachments) will be copied.

- Choose **R**emove local version of documents older than to enter the number of days you want to keep documents.

But I Set It Up   The mail settings just described only affect NotesMail. If you are using a mail system other than NotesMail, check the documentation for that mail system.

A remote connection document must be set up to make the connection between the server and your computer. It is also used to set up regularly scheduled exchanges of data. You can check (and possibly change) the information in an existing Remote Connection document through your personal Name & Address Book database under the view Connections. The servers shown are those that can be accessed.

If you must create a remote connection document, follow these steps:

1. Open your personal Name & Address Book.

2. Choose Compose Connection Remote. Then identify the server, port, and phone number.

You can also identify regularly scheduled calling (if appropriate), along with any connection script information to identify special characters to send after the server connection is established.

As you've seen, there is a good deal of setup activity to complete before you are ready to call the server. The good news is that once the setup is complete, it is usually done for good.

Connecting and Disconnecting

You may want to connect with the server to work interactively on the shared databases stored there or to replicate (exchange) database information with your local replica databases.

To call the Notes server to work interactively and/or make database replicas, follow these steps:

1. Choose Tools Call.

2. The Call Server dialog box appears (see Figure 18.1). Select a server from the Server list (which shows the servers in the remote connection documents in your personal Name & Address Book). Make sure the Phone Number and Port are entered correctly. Identify any other options to use. Generally, you will make few, if any, changes in this dialog box.

3. Select Auto Dial to dial through the modem rather than having to manually pick up the phone to dial.

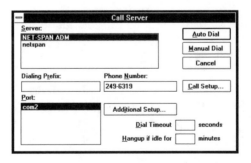

Figure 18.1   The Call Server dialog box.

When the connection is made, the Notes workspace appears. You may work interactively or create a replica database. See the next section, "Using Replica Databases," for more details on the latter.

To quit the dial-up session, select Tools Hangup. The Hang Up dialog box appears. Make sure the port is selected and select Hangup.

Using Replica Databases

Before you can replicate (exchange) a database with the server, local replicas of the databases must be set up. Once the replica database is set up, you can exchange data. If you selected Dial-up Workstation during Notes setup, the mail replica database is already set up for you and appears in the workspace. If you intend to work interactively on the server's databases, you do not have to replicate databases.

Creating a Replica Database

Follow these steps to create a replica database:

1. Choose File New Replica.

2. Figure 18.2 shows the New Replica dialog box. Enter the Original Database Server and Filename (database) from which to make the replica. (Databases have a file extension of NSF.) Enter the same information as appropriate for the New Replica.

3. Leave the Replicate Access Control List checked so you can replicate your changes to the server if desired. You can also limit the replication by checking and

entering the days in the text box labeled Only replicate documents saved in the last xx days.

4. Select Initialize and Copy Now to begin the replication.

5. Select New.

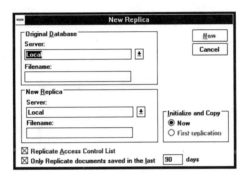

Figure 18.2   The New Replica dialog box.

Replicating Databases

Once replica databases are set up on your local workstation, you can call the Notes server to exchange data between local replica databases and server shared databases. Follow these steps:

1. Select the database(s) to replicate if you don't want to replicate all databases in common.

2. Select Tools Replicate.

3. In the Tools Replicate dialog box (Figure 18.3), select the Notes Server and other options desired. Generally, you'll want to replicate all databases (unless you've

selected databases), receive and send documents, transfer outgoing mail, and hang up when done.

4. Select **OK**.

5. A message will appear to confirm the call. Select **Yes**.

6. The Call Sever dialog box appears. Select **Auto Dial** to dial with the modem rather than manually with the telephone.

Figure 18.3 The Tools Replicate dialog box.

Too Big Your dial-up workstation may not have enough space to store sizeable databases. For that reason, it is important to limit the size of the database when it is replicated and to delete unnecessary documents. If you choose to delete documents you don't need, protect the server when you replicate. Select the database then choose **File Database Information Replication**. In the Replicate Settings dialog box, select **Do not replicate deletions to replicas of this database**. This way, deletions you make will not affect the shared database on the server.

Handling Mail

You will have a mail database set up on the server that you can replicate on the remote workstation. If you selected Dial-up Workstation during the setup of Notes, a mail database was set up on your computer. If you selected LAN Workstation, you must create a local replica of your mail database following the steps described earlier in this lesson.

Once a local mail database is set up, you must call the Notes server to initially replicate your mail database on the server using the steps covered earlier.

When you compose mail, you will do it in your Mail database. The Outgoing Mail database is simply a temporary storage area to hold mail to be sent. (To learn more about composing mail, see Lesson 12.)

Sending mail is just like replicating any database. To send mail, select Tools Replicate and make sure Transfer outgoing mail is checked. Select OK.

Lesson 19

Application Development

In this lesson, you will learn the process for developing new applications and changing existing applications and, if you have the proper access, the basics of creating and customizing a new database.

Application Design and Maintenance

You may want a new Notes database application for the work you perform or you may need to add changes to an existing application. Either option leads you into the world of application design and maintenance. This lesson introduces you to that world so you can see the role you'll play, as well as the work that's typically involved.

Most organizations have application designers who specialize in designing Notes applications. These application designers work with the intended clients of the application (that's you, the end user) from the initial needs assessment through implementing the final application. How long will it take? That depends on the scope of the work. Simple changes can be performed in a short period of time, while the initial development of complex database applications involving many clients takes much longer.

Whether you become involved in a process to create or to change an application, the steps of the process are the same. For simple changes, the steps can be performed quickly and informally. For complex, large application development, the steps will take longer, be more formal, and may include documented client sign-offs at several points.

The first step is *planning*. During planning, the designer works with the clients to identify the business needs and to verify that an application can be built or changed to meet those needs. Planning also includes a definition of the views and forms that would be required along with technical requirements. The client must verify the plan to make sure it meets the original business requirements.

The Excellent Client   Be an excellent client. A poor strategy is not knowing what you want, not consulting a representative sample of application users, and constantly changing the approach. Excellent clients know the goals of the application, make sure it meets everyone's needs as much as possible, and stick with a consistent approach.

After analysis comes *design specification*. This step takes the agreed-upon plan to a detailed level. The field names, lengths, and types are identified and views are designed. Detailed technical information is determined. Although many of the technical issues seem unimportant (if not incomprehensible) to the client, they are of great importance in making a Notes database run. The more a client can learn about Notes options at this point, the better for achieving the application desired. Also, if changes are required, clients must speak up now or forever hold their peace. (Once the next step has begun, it is much more difficult and costly to make changes.) The client usually has to approve the design specification before proceeding to the next step.

Once the design is in place, *development* of the Notes database begins. This includes creation of the forms and views, testing of the application, and development of the documentation. The client must stay involved and make incremental reviews of the work as it progresses. Clients are often requested to test portions of the development as they are completed.

Once the application is created or modified, that's it. Right? Wrong. Now comes *roll out* when all clients are assigned access to the application, training is conducted, and the application is used in the "real world." There is also a follow-up with the clients to determine if problems exist and, if so, to get them corrected.

Doing It Yourself

Developing a large application is a complex and time-consuming process. There are two easy ways to develop a new database. One is to use a template (a database without data documents) and then add data documents. A second approach is to copy an existing database and edit the data documents included. After you've created a new database, you can use it "as is" or have modifications made to better fit your needs.

If you choose to create a new application from an existing template or database, always do it on your local hard disk by identifying the server as "local." When you are sure the database is to your liking, work with the Notes Administrator to have user access set up and to copy the database to the server.

The following sections provide instructions on how to create a database using a template and how to copy an existing database. These instructions are only intended to whet your appetite for more. Consult the Notes documentation for complete development information.

Not Everyone Can You will only be able to perform the steps in this section if you have appropriate access rights.

Using an Existing Template

Notes comes with templates for creating common applications. For example, there is a template for reservation scheduling, news distribution, document library, service request tracking, and even a "to do" list. You might even be able to use a Notes supplied template "as is" to create a useful database for your organization.

To use a template to create a new database, follow these steps:

1. Choose File New Database (or press Ctrl+N).

2. In the New Database dialog box (see Figure 19.1), select the Server where the database will be stored (use local to place the database on your hard disk for further work). Enter the Filename for the database (eight characters or less) and a Title. Select the Design Server on which the template is located and select the Template. (Use the About button to see a description of the template.) Make sure Inherit Design is checked.

3. Select the New button. The database is created.

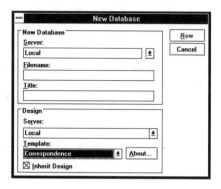

Figure 19.1   The New Database dialog box.

Creating a Template or Copying a Database

If you are using a custom designed database that someone else would like to adapt for his or her own use, you can create a template from the database that omits the data documents. Another alternative is to copy an entire database and then edit the data documents as you like.

NTF Files   When you create a template or a database, the resulting file name must be eight characters or less and have the extension *NTF*. For example, you could call a database meant for time reporting TIMERPT.NTF.

To make a template file from an existing database or to copy a database, follow these steps:

1. Select the database and choose File Database Copy.

2. From the Database Copy dialog box (shown in Figure 19.2), select the Server on which to store the new

146

database (use local for your hard disk). Enter an eight character or less Filename for the database with an NTF extension and a Title. To create a template, select Forms and Views Only. To make a copy of the entire database, choose Forms, Views, and Documents. Deselect Access Control List.

3. Select the New Copy button.

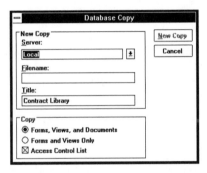

Figure 19.2   The Database Copy dialog box.

I Got It   When you create a template or copy a database, an icon for the new database will be placed on your workspace. If you only intended to create the file for someone else to use, you can remove the icon from your workspace. To do so, select the icon and choose Edit Clear (or press Delete or select the SmartIcon). Don't use File Database Delete unless you want to delete the entire file, not just the icon.

Customizing a Database

Once you have a new database, you may want to customize it. For example, the Using Database document describes how to use the database. The About Database document covers descriptive information like the who, what, when, where, and why of the database. To edit either document, select the database. Choose Design Help Document. Then choose either Using Database or About Database. Edit and save the document.

Customizing forms, views, and icons is also handled through the Design menu. The steps involved are considerably more complex than simply editing one of the help documents. To learn how to perform this advanced design work, consult the Notes documentation.

Remember, once the database is set up, you will need to work with the Notes Administrator to roll it out. The Notes Administrator will set up the access control list (to identify who has access to the database) and will copy the database to the server.

In this lesson, you learned the steps involved in developing Notes applications, as well as how to create new databases. You also learned the basics about performing simple customizations.

Appendix A
Microsoft Windows Primer

Microsoft Windows is an interface program that makes your computer easier to use by enabling you to select menu items and pictures rather than type commands. Before you can take advantage of it, however, you must learn some Windows basics.

Starting Microsoft Windows

To start Windows, do the following:

1. At the DOS prompt, type win.

2. Press Enter.

The Windows title screen appears for a few moments, and then you see a screen like the one in Figure A.1.

What If It Didn't Work? You may have to change to the Windows directory before starting Windows; to do so, type CD \WINDOWS and press Enter.

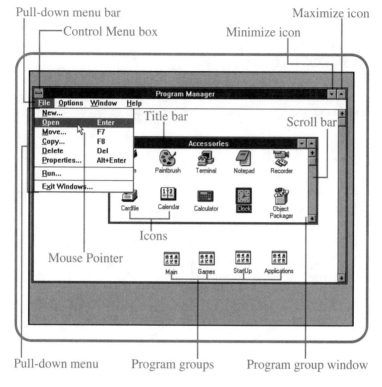

Pull-down menu bar

Control Menu box

Maximize icon

Minimize icon

Figure A.1   The Windows Program Manager.

Parts of a Windows Screen

As shown in Figure A.1, the Windows screen contains several unique elements that you won't see in DOS. Here's a brief summary.

- *Title bar*   Shows the name of the window or program.

- *Program group windows*   Contains program icons which allow you to run programs.

150

- *Icons*   Graphic representations of programs. To run a program, you select its icon.

- *Minimize and Maximize buttons*   Alters a window's size. The Minimize button shrinks the window to the size of an icon. The Maximize button expands the window to fill the screen. When maximized, a window contains a double-arrow *Restore* button, which returns the window to its original size.

- *Control Menu box*   Pulls down a menu that offers size and location controls for the window.

- *Pull-down menu bar*   Contains a list of the pull-down menus available in the program.

- *Mouse pointer*   If you are using a mouse, the mouse pointer (usually an arrow) appears on-screen. It can be controlled by moving the mouse (discussed in the next section).

- *Scroll bars*   If a window contains more information than can be displayed in the window, a scroll bar appears. *Scroll arrows* on each end of the scroll bar allow you to scroll slowly. The *scroll box* allows you to scroll more quickly.

Using a Mouse

To work most efficiently in Windows, you should use a mouse. You can press mouse buttons and move the mouse in various ways to change the way it acts:

> *Point* means to move the mouse pointer onto the specified item by moving the mouse. The tip of the mouse pointer must be touching the item.

Click on an item means to move the pointer onto the specified item and press the mouse button once. Unless specified otherwise, use the left mouse button.

Double-click on an item means to move the pointer onto the specified item and press and release the mouse button twice quickly.

Drag means to move the mouse pointer onto the specified item, hold down the mouse button, and move the mouse while holding down the button.

Starting a Program

To start a program, simply select its icon. If its icon is contained in a program group window that's not open at the moment, open the window first. Follow these steps:

1. If necessary, open the program group window that contains the program you want to run. To open a program group window, click on its icon.

2. Double-click on the icon for the program you want to run.

Using Menus

The pull-down menu bar (shown in Figure A.3) contains various menus from which you can select commands. Each Windows program that you run has a set of pull-down menus; Windows itself has a set too.

To open a menu, click on its name on the menu bar. Once a menu is open, you can select a command from it by clicking on the desired command.

Accelerator Keys Notice that in Figure A.2, some commands are followed by key names such as Enter (for the **O**pen command) or F8 (for the **C**opy command). These are called *accelerator keys*. You can use these keys to perform the commands without even opening the menu.

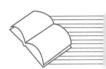

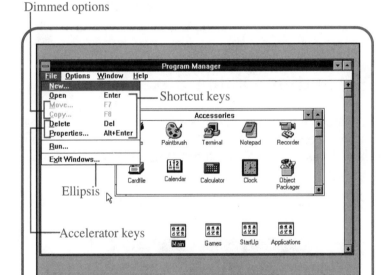

Figure A.2 A menu lists various commands you can perform.

153

Usually, when you select a command, the command is performed immediately. However:

- If the command name is gray (rather than black), the command is unavailable at the moment and you cannot choose it.

- If the command name is followed by an arrow, selecting the command will cause another menu to appear, from which you select another command.

- If the command name is followed by an ellipsis (three dots), selecting it will cause a dialog box to appear. You'll learn about dialog boxes in the next section.

Navigating Dialog Boxes

A dialog box is Windows' way of requesting additional information. For example, if you choose Properties from the File menu, you'll see the dialog box shown in Figure A.3.

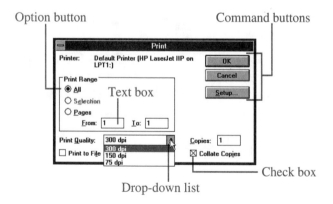

Figure A.3 A typical dialog box.

Each dialog box contains one or more of the following elements:

* *List boxes* display available choices. To activate a list, click inside the list box. If the entire list is not visible, use the scroll bar to view the items in the list. To select an item from the list, click on it.

* *Drop-down lists* are similar to list boxes, but only one item in the list is shown. To see the rest of the items, click on the down arrow to the right of the list box. To select an item from the list, click on it.

* *Text boxes* allow you to type an entry. To activate a text box, click inside it. To edit an existing entry, use the arrow keys to move the cursor, and the Delete or Backspace keys to delete existing characters, and then type your correction.

* *Check boxes* allow you to select one or more items in a group of options. For example, if you are styling text, you may select Bold and Italic to have the text appear in both bold and italic type. Click on a check box to activate it.

* *Option buttons* are like check boxes, but you can select only one option button in a group. Selecting one button unselects any option that is already selected. Click on an option button to activate it.

* *Command buttons* execute (or cancel) the command once you have made your selections in the dialog box. To press a command button, click on it.

Switching Between Windows

Many times you will have more than one window open at once. Some open windows may be program group windows, while others may be actual programs that are running. To switch among them, you can:

- Pull down the Window menu and choose the window you want to view

  or

- If a portion of the desired window is visible, click on it.

Controlling a Window

As you saw earlier in this appendix, you can minimize, maximize, and restore windows on your screen. But you can also move them and change their size.

- To move a window, drag its title bar to a different location. (Remember, "drag" means to hold down the left mouse button while you move the mouse.)

- To resize a window, position the mouse pointer on the border of the window until you see a double-headed arrow; then drag the window border to the desired size.

Copying Your Program Diskettes with File Manager

Before you install any new software, you should make a copy of the original diskettes as a safety precaution. Windows' File Manager makes this process easy.

First, start File Manager by double-clicking on the File Manager icon in the Main program group. Then for each disk you need to copy, follow these steps:

1. Locate a blank disk of the same type as the original disk, and label it to match the original. Make sure the disk you select does not contain any data that you want to keep.

2. Place the original disk in your diskette drive (A or B).

3. Open the Disk menu and select Copy Disk. The Copy Disk dialog box appears.

4. Select the drive used in step 2 from the Source In list box.

5. Select the same drive from the Destination In list box. (Don't worry, File Manager will tell you to switch disks at the appropriate time.)

6. Select OK. The Confirm Copy Disk dialog box appears.

7. Select Yes to continue.

8. When instructed to insert the Source diskette, choose OK, since you already did this at step 2. The Copying Disk box appears, and the copy process begins.

9. When instructed to insert the target disk, remove the original disk from the drive and insert the blank disk. Then choose OK to continue. The Copying Disk box disappears when the process is complete.

Index

159

D

E

F